# SMP interact

## for GCSE mathematics

## Practice for Higher

CAMBRIDGE UNIVERSITY PRESS

PUBLISHED BY THE PRESS SYNDICATE OF THE UNIVERSITY OF CAMBRIDGE
The Pitt Building, Trumpington Street, Cambridge, United Kingdom

CAMBRIDGE UNIVERSITY PRESS
The Edinburgh Building, Cambridge CB2 2RU, UK
40 West 20th Street, New York, NY 10011-4211, USA
477 Williamstown Road, Port Melbourne, VIC 3207, Australia
Ruiz de Alarcón 13, 28014 Madrid, Spain
Dock House, The Waterfront, Cape Town 8001, South Africa

http://www.cambridge.org/

© The School Mathematics Project 2003
First published 2003

Printed in the United Kingdom at the University Press, Cambridge

*Typeface* Minion   *System* QuarkXPress®

*A catalogue record for this book is available from the British Library*

ISBN 0 521 89024 1 paperback

Typesetting and technical illustrations by The School Mathematics Project
Cover image © Getty Images/Nick Koudis
Cover design by Angela Ashton

# Contents

## 2 *The tangent function*

### Section A

**1** Find the opposite sides in these right-angled triangles.
Give your answers correct to two decimal places.

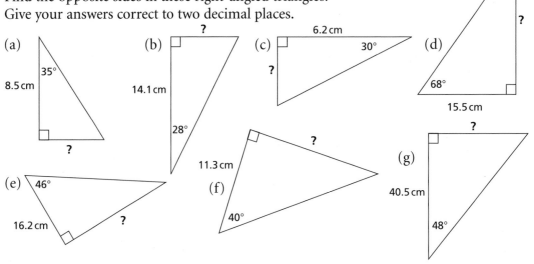

(a) 35° 8.5 cm ?

(b) ? 14.1 cm 28°

(c) 6.2 cm 30° ?

(d) ? 68° 15.5 cm

(e) 46° 16.2 cm ?

(f) 11.3 cm 40°

(g) ? 40.5 cm 48°

?

### Section B

**1** Find the adjacent sides in these right-angled triangles, correct to 2 d.p.

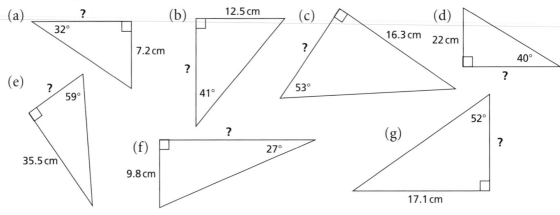

(a) ? 32° 7.2 cm

(b) 12.5 cm 41° ?

(c) ? 16.3 cm 53°

(d) 22 cm 40° ?

(e) ? 59° 35.5 cm

(f) ? 9.8 cm 27°

(g) 52° ? 17.1 cm

**2** Find the missing sides, to 2 d.p. Some are opposite and some are adjacent.

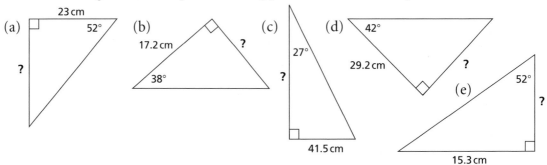

(a) 23 cm 52° ?

(b) 17.2 cm 38° ?

(c) 27° 41.5 cm ?

(d) 42° 29.2 cm ?

(e) 52° 15.3 cm ?

## Section C

**1** Find the angle marked with a letter in each of these triangles, to the nearest 0.1°.

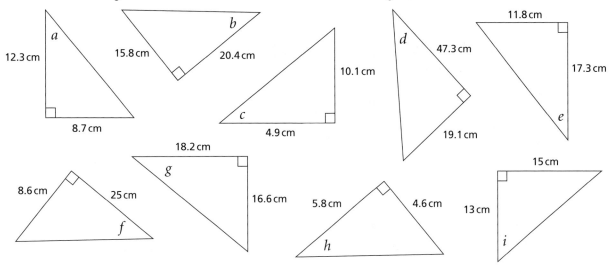

## Section D

**1** Find the missing lengths and angles in these right-angled triangles.

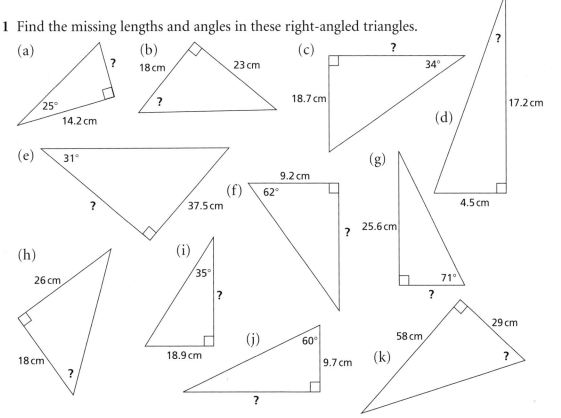

**2** The diagram shows the end view of a ridge tent.
Calculate the length of the base.

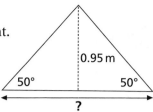

**3** The coordinates of the vertices of triangle ABC are A (2, 5), B (6, 12) and C (6, 5).
Find angle CAB.

**4** A tower is 21 m high.
Point R is 45 m from the base of the tower.

Calculate the angle of elevation
of the top of the tower from R.

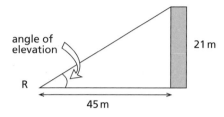

**5** Zara starts from A, walks 9 km east to B
and then walks 4 km south to C.
Find the bearing of C from A.

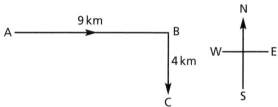

**6** XYZ is an isosceles triangle.
Find its area.

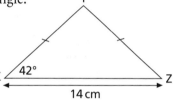

**7** The acute angle between the diagonals in this rectangle is 50°.
The shorter side of the rectangle is 10 cm.
Find the length of the longer side.

**8** Find the area of this rectangle.

**9** In this kite angle BAD = 74°.
Find angle BCD.

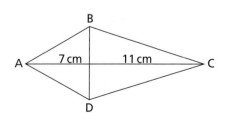

**10** Find the area of triangle PQR.

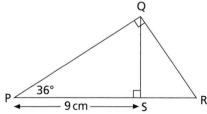

# 3 Fractions

## Sections A and B

1 Work these out.

(a) $\frac{3}{5} + \frac{1}{4}$      (b) $\frac{7}{8} - \frac{2}{5}$      (c) $\frac{9}{10} + \frac{1}{3}$      (d) $\frac{7}{9} - \frac{7}{10}$

(e) $1\frac{2}{3} + \frac{3}{5}$      (f) $2\frac{1}{2} - 1\frac{1}{3}$      (g) $3\frac{3}{4} - 1\frac{7}{10}$      (h) $4\frac{1}{3} - 2\frac{9}{10}$

2 Work these out.

(a) $\frac{2}{3} \times \frac{5}{8}$      (b) $\frac{2}{5}$ of $\frac{2}{3}$      (c) $\frac{3}{4}$ of $\frac{8}{15}$      (d) $\frac{8}{15} \times \frac{6}{11}$

(e) $\frac{3}{4} \times 7$      (f) $8 \times \frac{7}{12}$      (g) $\frac{1}{5}$ of $2\frac{1}{2}$      (h) $\frac{2}{3} \times 1\frac{7}{8}$

3 $\frac{3}{5}$ of a number is 45. What is the number?

4 This sequence continues by adding the same fraction each time.
Find the next three numbers in the sequence.

$\frac{1}{3}$, $1\frac{1}{6}$, 2, ...

*5 A 'spiral' design is drawn so that each straight section is
three-quarters of the length of the previous section.

(a) If the first section is 32 units long, write down the
lengths of the first five sections.

(b) What is the total length of this five-section design?

## Sections C and D

1 Write down the reciprocal of

(a) 7      (b) $\frac{8}{15}$      (c) $\frac{1}{9}$      (d) 0.1      (e) $3\frac{1}{2}$

2 Work these out.

(a) $\frac{3}{4} \div \frac{5}{8}$      (b) $1\frac{1}{2} \div \frac{1}{4}$      (c) $6 \div \frac{2}{3}$      (d) $12 \div \frac{1}{3}$

(e) $\frac{1}{2} \div 3$      (f) $\frac{3}{10} \div 2$      (g) $2\frac{1}{2} \div \frac{2}{5}$      (h) $2\frac{1}{4} \div 1\frac{1}{2}$

3 At a dog kennels, 12 tins of dog food are shared out so that each dog gets $\frac{3}{4}$ of a tin.
How many dogs will this feed?

4 What fraction is halfway between

(a) $\frac{3}{10}$ and $\frac{1}{2}$      (b) $\frac{2}{3}$ and $\frac{3}{4}$      (c) $\frac{3}{5}$ and $1\frac{1}{4}$

## Section E

1 Work these out.

(a) $\frac{3}{7} + \frac{1}{2}$      (b) $\frac{5}{8} - \frac{2}{7}$      (c) $\frac{4}{9} - \frac{1}{6}$      (d) $\frac{5}{6} + \frac{2}{7}$

(e) $\frac{4}{5} \times \frac{2}{9}$      (f) $\frac{3}{4} \times \frac{5}{9}$      (g) $\frac{3}{4} \div \frac{5}{8}$      (h) $1\frac{1}{2} \div \frac{1}{4}$

2 If $\frac{5}{8}$ of a number is 40, what is the number?

3 King Loot taxed his subjects in the following way.

He took $\frac{1}{2}$ of a person's wealth as defence tax.

He then took $\frac{2}{3}$ of what was left as protection tax.

He then took $\frac{4}{5}$ of what was left as security tax.

One of his subjects had 7 crowns left after tax. How much tax did he pay?

4 In an election there were four candidates: Arjan, Bess, Colin and Diane.
Between 400 and 450 people voted.
Exactly $\frac{2}{5}$ voted for Arjan, $\frac{1}{3}$ for Bess and $\frac{1}{4}$ for Colin.

(a) How many people voted altogether?

(b) How many voted for Diane?

5 I am thinking of two fractions.
When I add them, I get $\frac{8}{15}$.
When I multiply them, I get $\frac{1}{24}$.
What do I get when I subtract the smaller fraction from the larger?

6 Solve these equations.

(a) $\frac{1}{6}x = \frac{5}{8}$      (b) $\frac{3}{4}x = \frac{7}{8}$      (c) $\frac{2}{5}x = \frac{6}{7}$      (d) $\frac{5}{8}x = \frac{1}{3}$

7 Jane turns on the hot tap of her bath and in 1 minute it fills $\frac{1}{10}$ of the bath.
She turns off the hot tap and turns on the cold tap.
After 1 more minute, the bath is $\frac{1}{6}$ full.

(a) What fraction of the bath does the cold tap fill in 1 minute?

(b) Jane now turns on the hot tap as well as the cold.
After how many more minutes will the bath be full?

8 Here are two ways of finding out whether one number, $A$, is larger than another, $B$.

(i) Work out $A - B$. If the result is positive, then $A > B$.

(ii) Work out $A \div B$. If the result is greater than 1, then $A > B$.

Use each of these methods to find out whether $\frac{5}{7}$ is larger or smaller than $\frac{3}{4}$.

# 4 Indices 1

## Section A

**1** Write these using index notation.

    (a) $2 \times 2 \times 2 \times 2$        (b) $10 \times 10 \times 10$        (c) $7 \times 7 \times 7 \times 7 \times 7$

**2** Calculate the value of each of these.

    (a) $2^6$        (b) $5^3$        (c) $10^4$        (d) $20^3$

**3** Calculate the value of each of these.

    (a) $12 + 3^2$       (b) $5^3 - 10^2$       (c) $7 \times 5^2$       (d) $5^3 \times 2^3$

**4** Which is bigger?

    (a) $2^{10}$ or $10^2$            (b) $5^4$ or $4^5$

**5** A piece of paper is folded in half so that it is 2 sheets thick.

    It is folded in half again so that it is 4 sheets thick.
    It is folded in half three more times.

    (a) How many sheets thick is it now?

    (b) Write your answer using index notation.

**6** In diagram 1 there are 3 ends identified by blobs.
    In diagram 2 there are 9 ends.

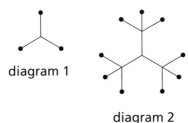

diagram 1

diagram 2

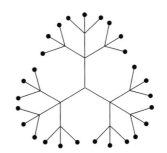

diagram 3

    (a) How many ends are there in diagram 3?

    (b) If you continued drawing the pattern, how many ends would there be in diagram 5?

    (c) Write down the number of ends in diagram 12 using index notation.

    (d) Write down an expression for the number of ends in diagram $n$.

**7** Arrange each set of numbers in order of size, starting with the smallest.

(a) $6^9$   $8^8$   $10^7$   $12^6$   $14^5$       (b) $2^{11}$   $3^7$   $5^5$   $7^4$

**8** Solve the following equations.

(a) $x^5 = 59\,049$       (b) $8^x = 4096$       (c) $x^8 = 5\,764\,801$

**✗ 9** There is an error in the end digit of each of these calculations.

Explain without using a calculator why each calculation cannot possibly be correct.

| | |
|---|---|
| (a) | $2^{21} = 2\,097\,153$ |
| (b) | $5^8 = 390\,623$ |
| (c) | $4^8 = 65\,530$ |
| (d) | $6^{10} = 60\,466\,174$ |

**10** The date 3 April 2081 can be written as 3/4/81.
This date is unusual as $3^4 = 81$.

2 March 2008 can be written as 2/3/08 and it is true that $2^3 = 8$.

Find at least four dates $d/m/y$ like this in the 21st century so that $d^m = y$.

## Section B

**1** Find the prime factorisation of each of these numbers and write it using index notation.

(a) 80       (b) 441       (c) 72       (d) 600

**2** 200 can be written as $2^x \times 5^y$.

Find $x$ and $y$.

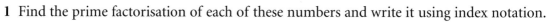

**3** 49 000 can be written as $2^r \times 5^s \times 7^t$.

Find $r$, $s$ and $t$.

**4** $207 = 3^2 \times 23$

Use this prime factorisation to find all six factors of 207.

**5** Use prime factorisation to find the LCM of

(a) 15 and 24       (b) 18 and 40       (c) 36 and 108       (d) 24, 30 and 80

**6** Use prime factorisation to find the HCF of

(a) 40 and 108       (b) 36 and 80       (c) 96 and 180       (d) 420 and 560

**7** A packet of sweets can be shared equally among 2 or 3 or 4 or 5 people.

What is the smallest number of sweets that could be in the packet?

**8** A cuboid 144 mm long, 126 mm wide and 108 mm tall is cut up into cubes all the same size.

(a) If there is no waste, what are the dimensions of the largest possible cube?

(b) How many of these cubes will there be?

# Section C

**1** Find the numbers missing from these calculations.

(a) $5^3 \times 5^2 = (5 \times 5 \times 5) \times (5 \times 5) = 5^\blacksquare$

(b) $\dfrac{10^5}{10^4} = \dfrac{10 \times 10 \times 10 \times 10 \times 10}{10 \times 10 \times 10 \times 10} = 10^\blacksquare$

(c) $4^4 \times 4^3 = (4 \times 4 \times 4 \times 4) \times (4 \times 4 \times 4) = 4^\blacksquare$

(d) $\dfrac{3^5}{3^2} = \dfrac{3 \times 3 \times 3 \times 3 \times 3}{3 \times 3} = 3^\blacksquare$

**2** Match each calculation with an answer.

| Calculation | Answer |
|---|---|
| (a) $7^4 \times 7^6$ | A: $7^9$ |
| (b) $7^{20} \div 7^8$ | B: $7^{10}$ |
| (c) $7^3 \times 7^3 \times 7^3$ | C: $7^{15}$ |
| (d) $(7^8 \times 7^9) \div 7^2$ | D: $7^{12}$ |

**3** Find the value of $\blacksquare$ in the following calculations.

(a) $2^3 \times 2^\blacksquare = 2^{12}$

(b) $10^6 \div 10^\blacksquare = 10^3$

(c) $a^\blacksquare \times a^5 = a^{20}$

(d) $\dfrac{c^\blacksquare \times c^3}{c^4} = c^8$

(e) $\dfrac{7^5 \times 7^4}{7^\blacksquare} = 7^3$

**4** Copy and complete these multiplication grids.

(a)

| $\times$ | | $2^3$ | |
|---|---|---|---|
| $2^5$ | $2^9$ | | |
| | $2^{10}$ | | |
| $2^8$ | | | $2^{10}$ |

(b)

| $\times$ | $b^4$ | | |
|---|---|---|---|
| | | $b^{11}$ | $b^{14}$ |
| $b^7$ | | | $b^{13}$ |
| | $b^9$ | | |

**5** Find the value of $x$ and $y$ in each statement.

(a) $2^3 \times 3^2 \times 2^4 = 2^x \times 3^y$

(b) $5^3 \times 3^2 \times 5^4 \times 3^6 = 5^x \times 3^y$

(c) $\dfrac{4^9 \times 3^6}{4^3 \times 3^4} = 4^x \times 3^y$

(d) $\dfrac{3^6 \times 5^9 \times 3^7}{5^4 \times 3^5 \times 5^3} = 3^x \times 5^y$

**6** Find the value of $n$ in each statement.

(a) $(3^4)^2 = 3^4 \times 3^4 = 3^n$

(b) $(7^3)^4 = 7^3 \times 7^3 \times 7^3 \times 7^3 = 7^n$

(c) $(5^3)^4 = 5^n$

(d) $(a^5)^3 = a^n$

**7** Find the value of $x$.

(a) $(3^2)^x = 3^8$

(b) $(2^x)^3 = 2^9$

(c) $(5^3)^2 = 5^x$

**8** Copy and complete these.

(a) $9^4 = (3^2)^4 = 3^\blacksquare$

(b) $8^5 = (2^\blacksquare)^5 = 2^\blacksquare$

(c) $81^3 = (3^\blacksquare)^3 = 3^\blacksquare$

(d) $125^2 = 5^\blacksquare$

(e) $64^3 = 4^\blacksquare$

(f) $27^5 = 3^\blacksquare$

11

⊠ **9** Find four pairs of equivalent expressions

$$4^4 \qquad 2^{12} \qquad 32^2 \qquad 4^9 \qquad 2^{10} \qquad 2^8 \qquad 8^4 \qquad 8^6$$

## Section D

**1** Simplify these.
(a) $3x^2 \times 5x^3$        (b) $3y^2 \times y^5$        (c) $2w \times 3w^2 \times 6w^3$
(d) $(3y^2)^4$        (e) $(2u^5)^3$        (f) $(v^2w^3)^5$

**2** Simplify these.
(a) $\dfrac{10x^5}{2x^3}$        (b) $\dfrac{8y^2}{16y^5}$        (c) $\dfrac{12v^4}{3v}$

(d) $\left(\dfrac{6x}{18x^3}\right)^2$        (e) $\left(\dfrac{8w^5}{4w^3}\right)^3$        (f) $\dfrac{8x^3 \times 3y^2}{6x^2 \times 4y^3}$

**3** Copy and complete these multiplication grids.

(a)
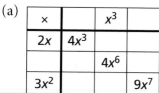

| × |  | $x^3$ |  |
|---|---|---|---|
| $2x$ | $4x^3$ |  |  |
|  |  | $4x^6$ |  |
| $3x^2$ |  |  | $9x^7$ |

(b)

| × |  |  | $2y^3$ |
|---|---|---|---|
| $5y$ |  |  |  |
| $2y^3$ |  | $4y^7$ |  |
|  | $3y^4$ |  | $2y^5$ |

## Section E

**1** What is the value of $5^0$?

**2** Copy and complete these.
(a) $\dfrac{1}{4} = \dfrac{1}{2^\blacksquare} = 2^\blacksquare$      (b) $\dfrac{1}{27} = \dfrac{1}{3^\blacksquare} = 3^\blacksquare$      (c) $\dfrac{1}{64} = 4^\blacksquare$

(d) $\dfrac{1}{1000} = 10^\blacksquare$      (e) $5^{-3} = \dfrac{1}{5^\blacksquare}$      (f) $\dfrac{1}{32} = 3^\blacksquare$

**3** Write the reciprocals of the following in the form $2^n$.
(a) $2^5$     (b) $4^2$     (c) $2^0$     (d) $2^{-4}$     (e) $8^2$

⊠ **4** Write the following as decimals.
(a) $10^{-1}$     (b) $\dfrac{1}{10^3}$     (c) $10^{-5}$     (d) $10^{-8}$     (e) $10^{-4}$

**5** Write the following as decimals correct to three significant figures.

(a) $7^{-1}$    (b) $6^{-2}$    (c) $\dfrac{5^2}{3^5}$    (d) $9^{-2}$    (e) $5 \times 3^{-2}$

**6** Solve these.

(a) $2^x = \dfrac{1}{8}$    (b) $5^x = 5$    (c) $4^x = 0.25$    (d) $\dfrac{1}{3^x} = 1$

(e) $x^{-3} = 0.125$    (f) $10^x = 0.01$    (g) $x^{-4} = \dfrac{1}{81}$    (h) $8^5 = \dfrac{1}{2^x}$

## Section F

**1** Find the value of $n$ in each statement.

(a) $2^5 \times 2^{-3} = 2^n$    (b) $7^{-5} \times 7^3 = 7^n$    (c) $3^0 \times 3^4 = 3^n$

(d) $5^{-2} \times 5^0 = 5^n$    (e) $5^{-2} \times 5^{-3} = 5^n$    (f) $10^{-4} \times 10^{-3} = 10^n$

**2** Copy and complete these.

(a) $\dfrac{2^3}{2^5} = 2^{\blacksquare}$    (b) $\dfrac{3^0}{3^5} = 3^{\blacksquare}$    (c) $\dfrac{5^2}{5^0} = 5^{\blacksquare}$    (d) $\dfrac{2^{-4}}{2^5} = 2^{\blacksquare}$

(e) $\dfrac{3^{-2}}{3^{-5}} = 3^{\blacksquare}$    (f) $\dfrac{2^3}{2^{\blacksquare}} = 2^0$    (g) $\dfrac{5^{-2}}{5^{\blacksquare}} = 5^{-3}$    (h) $\dfrac{7^{\blacksquare}}{7^6} = 7^3$

**3** Write the answers to the following in the form $3^n$.

(a) $(3^0)^3$    (b) $(3^{-2})^3$    (c) $(3^5)^0$    (d) $(3^3)^{-4}$

(e) $(3^{-2})^{-3}$    (f) $(9^2)^{-3}$    (g) $(27^{-1})^2$    (h) $(9^{-3})^{-2}$

**4** Copy and complete these multiplication grids.

(a)

| $\times$ | | $5^{-2}$ | |
|---|---|---|---|
| | | $5^{-6}$ | |
| $5^2$ | | | $5^2$ |
| $5^{-1}$ | $5^2$ | | |

(b)

| $\times$ | | $y^3$ | $y^{-4}$ |
|---|---|---|---|
| | 1 | | $y^{-1}$ |
| 1 | | | |
| | | 1 | |

**5** Simplify these.

(a) $x^3 \times x^{-5}$    (b) $x^{-2} \times x^{-3}$    (c) $3x^3 \times 5x^{-2}$    (d) $x^2 \times x^{-4} \times x^3$

(e) $\dfrac{x^5}{x^{-2}}$    (f) $\dfrac{x^{-4}}{x^5}$    (g) $\dfrac{5x^7}{10x^8}$    (h) $\dfrac{x^3 \times x^{-4}}{x^2}$

**6** Copy and complete these.

(a) $(x^2)^{-3} = x^{\blacksquare}$    (b) $(x^{\blacksquare})^4 = x^{-12}$    (c) $(x^{-2})^0 = x^{\blacksquare}$

(d) $(x^{\blacksquare})^{-4} = x^0$    (e) $(x^{-5})^{\blacksquare} = x^{15}$    (f) $(x^{-2})^{-3} = x^{\blacksquare}$

# 5 Forming and solving equations

## Section A

1 Solve each of these equations.

Check that your answer works in the original equation.

(a) $2x + 6 = 3 - x$

(b) $3x - 2 = 5 - 4x$

(c) $7 - 5x = 4x - 11$

(d) $8x + 2 = 3x - 8$

(e) $3x - 5 = 7 + 9x$

(f) $7x + 5 = 7 + 3x$

2 Solve each of these equations.

(a) $3x - 5 = 3 - 9x$

(b) $3 - 2x = 9 + 10x$

(c) $4 - 5x = 3x + 20$

(d) $8x - 9 = 6 + 2x$

(e) $5 - 23x = 11 - 5x$

(f) $1.5 - 9x = 5 - 2x$

3 Solve each of these equations.

(a) $9 - \frac{1}{2}x = 15 + x$

(b) $\frac{1}{8}x - 12 = 13 - \frac{1}{2}x$

(c) $\frac{5}{6}x - 5 = \frac{1}{2}x - 6$

(d) $3 - \frac{x}{14} = 9 - \frac{x}{2}$

(e) $\frac{2}{15}x + 19 = 7 - \frac{2}{3}x$

(f) $1 - \frac{x}{4} = 7 - \frac{x}{2}$

## Section B

1 Solve each of these equations.

(a) $2(x + 3) = 10$
(b) $9(x - 1) = 36$
(c) $12(x + 3) = {}^-12$
(d) $5(3x - 2) = 35$

2 Solve these.

(a) $3(x + 3) = 15 + x$

(b) $2(x - 6) = 5x - 6$

(c) $3(4x - 1) = 2(1 + x)$

(d) $2(5x + 6) = 3(2x + 5)$
(e) $2(x + 2) = x - 4$

(f) $2(5x - 1) = 7(x + 4)$

3 Solve these.

(a) $\frac{x-3}{4} = 1$

(b) $\frac{3x+2}{5} = 4$

(c) $\frac{5x-3}{7} = 6$

(d) $\frac{8-2x}{5} = 3$

(e) $\frac{9x+1}{2} = 14$

(f) $\frac{20-4x}{3} = 7$

4 Solve these.

(a) $5(3 - x) + 7(x - 2) = 9$

(b) $3(2x - 1) + 5(3x + 2) = 49$

(c) $3(4x - 1) - 2(3x + 2) = 17$

(d) $8(2x + 1) + 4(x + 4) = 16$

(e) $4(2x + 3) - 5(3x + 2) = 9$

5 Solve these.

(a) $\frac{3x+1}{2} = 2x - 3$

(b) $\frac{5x-2}{3} = 3x - 10$

(c) $\frac{6-2x}{4} = 19 + 3x$

(d) $2(3x + 3) + 5(2x + 5) = 63$

(e) $4(3x + 1) - 3(5 - 4x) = 1$

(f) $6(4x - 3) - 3(5 - 2x) = 57$

## Section C

1 Solve each of these equations.

(a) $\frac{3x+3}{4} = \frac{5x-6}{3}$

(b) $\frac{6x-2}{3} = \frac{8x+2}{5}$

(c) $\frac{4x+3}{5} = \frac{5x+2}{6}$

(d) $\frac{1}{2}(6x-3) = \frac{1}{5}(8x+3)$

2 Solve these.

(a) $\frac{5x-3}{2} - \frac{2x+1}{3} = 11$

(b) $\frac{6x+1}{2} - \frac{4x+1}{3} = 2x$

(c) $\frac{3x+2}{4} - 3(x-5) = \frac{x}{3}$

(d) $8 - \frac{x}{5} = 2(x-7)$

## Section D

1 Find the size of each angle in these shapes.

(a)

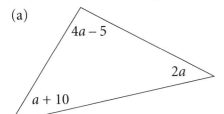

(b)

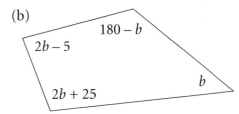

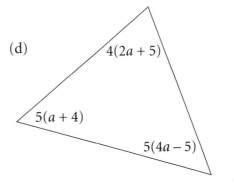

(c)

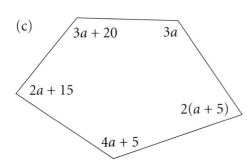

(d)

2 The perimeter of each of these shapes is 120 cm.
Find the length of each side.

(a)

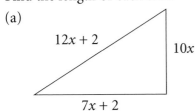

(b)

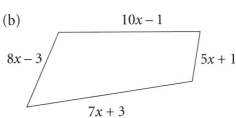

(c)

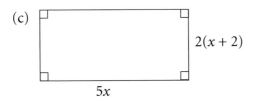

**3** Work out the starting number in each of these 'think of a number' puzzles.

(a) I think of a number.
I subtract 8 and multiply by 6.

My answer is double the number I first thought of.

(b) I think of a number.
I subtract 2 then multiply by 4 and take off 1.

My answer is 3 times the number I first thought of.

(c) Jack and Alex both think of the same number.

Jack subtracts 8 and then multiplies the result by 5.
Alex halves his number and then adds 14.

They both end up with the same number.

(d) Narinder and Brian both think of the same number.

Narinder subtracts 5 from her number and divides the result by 7.
Brian divides his number by 2 and then subtracts 10.

They both end up with the same number.

## Section E

**1** Solve these equations.

(a) $3x + 2 - 4(3 - x) = 18$  (b) $12 - 3x = 5x + 2$

(c) $\frac{1}{3}(x - 4) = \frac{3}{5}$  (d) $\frac{1}{2}(2x + 3) + \frac{2}{3}(2 - x) = 1$

**2** Harry is solving the equation $\frac{9}{x} = 18$.

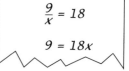
$$\frac{9}{x} = 18$$
$$9 = 18x$$

Copy and complete his working to find the value of $x$.

**3** Solve these equations.

(a) $\frac{20}{x} = 5$  (b) $\frac{20}{x} = 100$  (c) $\frac{8}{x} = 24$  (d) $\frac{4}{x} = 5$

**4** The area of this triangle is $40\,\text{cm}^2$.
Form an equation in $x$ and solve it.

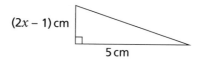
$(2x - 1)\,\text{cm}$

$5\,\text{cm}$

**5** The mean of the three numbers $(x - 3)$, $(x + 2)$ and $(2x - 11)$ is 10.
Form an equation and solve it to find the value of $x$.

**6** The perimeters of the rectangle and the equilateral triangle are equal.
Find the value of $x$.

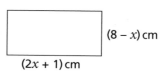
$(8 - x)\,\text{cm}$

$(2x + 1)\,\text{cm}$

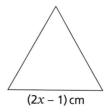
$(2x - 1)\,\text{cm}$

# Mixed questions 1

1 Sadia is carrying out a survey of opinions about school lunches in her class.
She gives a questionnaire to all the pupils in the class.
Here are some of the questions she asks.

| | |
|---|---|
| (a) How often do you have a school lunch? Please tick. | Never ...... Sometimes ...... Always ...... |
| (b) How long do you usually have to wait in the queue? | A short time ...... A long time ...... |
| (c) Do you think that the canteen should offer more vegetarian options, which are more healthy than meat? | Yes ...... No ...... |

Say whether you think each of these questions is satisfactory.
If it is unsatisfactory, suggest a way of improving it.

2 Calculate the sides and angles marked with letters.

(a)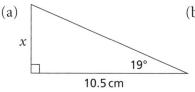

(b)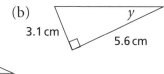

(c)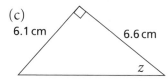

3 Solve these equations.

(a) $5(2 + x) = 7x + 9$     (b) $3x = 2(1 - x)$     (c) $7x = 4(2x - 1) - 3(x + 1)$

4 Simplify these expressions.

(a) $2a^4 \times 3a^3$   (b) $\dfrac{8a^7}{2a^4}$   (c) $4a^{-2} \times 5a^6$   (d) $2a^2 \times 5a^{-6}$   (e) $(3a^2)^{-3}$

5 If $r = \frac{3}{5}$ and $t = \frac{2}{3}$, find the value of

(a) $r + t$   (b) $rt$   (c) $\dfrac{r}{t}$   (d) $t^2$   (e) $4t$

6 Find the value of $n$ so that

(a) $5^n = 1$   (b) $5^n = 125$   (c) $5^n = \frac{1}{25}$   (d) $5^n = 0.2$   (e) $(5^2)^n = 5^8$

7 This diagram shows the end wall of a shed.
Calculate the length marked $l$.

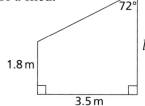

8 Solve these equations.   (a) $\frac{1}{5}x = \frac{3}{10}$   (b) $\frac{2}{3}x = \frac{4}{5}$   (c) $\frac{7}{8}x = \frac{3}{5}$   (d) $\frac{3}{4}x - \frac{2}{5} = 0$

9 (a) Find the prime factorisation of 60 and write it using index notation.

(b) Use prime factorisation to find the lowest common multiple of 60 and 48.

(c) Use prime factorisation to find the highest common factor of 60 and 105.

10 Solve these equations.

(a) $\dfrac{p-7}{3} = \dfrac{3p}{2}$

(b) $\dfrac{y+2}{3} - \dfrac{y+5}{5} = 1$

11 The members of a club can be either senior or junior.
The ratio of seniors to juniors in the club is $7:9$.
The ratio of males to females in the club is $5:7$.

(a) The club has fewer than 60 members.
How many members does it have?

(b) Which of these fractions is greater?
A: The fraction of club members who are males
B: The fraction of club members who are seniors

(c) One-eighth of the members are senior males.
How many junior females are there?

12 Solve these equations.

(a) $\dfrac{x}{3} = 15$

(b) $\dfrac{60}{x} = 15$

(c) $\dfrac{7}{x} = 14$

(d) $\dfrac{100}{x} = 1000$

13 (a) Use Pythagoras to find length $a$.

(b) Write down the value of $\tan x$.

(c) If $\tan y = 1.4$, work out length $b$.

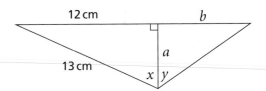

14 Triangle ABC is known to be isosceles,
but it is not known which two sides are equal.

(a) Find the three possible values of $x$.

(b) For each value of $x$ find the lengths
of the sides of the triangle.

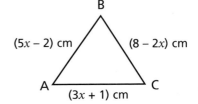

15 The diagram shows four squares 'nested' inside each other,
with each square formed by joining the midpoints
of the sides of the previous square.

(a) What fraction is the area of the fourth square
of the largest square?

(b) The process continues until there are $n$ squares.
Write down an expression for the fraction that
the $n$th square is of the largest square.

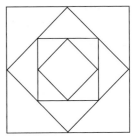

# 6 Rates

## Section A

1  Calculate the average speed, in m.p.h., of the following journeys.

(a)  220 miles in 4 hours                (b)  17 miles in 20 minutes

(c)  140 miles in $2\frac{1}{2}$ hours                (d)  48 miles in 45 minutes

(e)  65 miles in 1 hour 15 minutes    (f)  55 miles in 1 hour 50 minutes

2  Calculate the average speed, in kilometres per hour, when travelling

(a)  4 km in 6 minutes                (b)  32 km in 48 minutes

(c)  56 km in 35 minutes                (d)  half a kilometre in 4 minutes

3  A train left for a 70 mile journey at 10:15 and arrived at its destination at 11:30.
It then immediately returned, arriving back at 13:15.

(a)  What was the average speed of the train on its outward journey?

(b)  What was the average speed of the train on its return journey?

(c)  What was its average speed for the 140 mile round trip?

4  (a)  A sprinter can run 100 m in 10 seconds. What is his average speed in km/h?

(b)  An ostrich can run 200 m in 12 seconds. What is its average speed in km/h?

## Section B

1  The solid line on the graph shows
the 10 km journey of cyclist A.

(a)  What is the speed of cyclist A, in km/h?

(b)  Another cyclist B starts from the same
place and travels at 15 km/h.
At what time should she leave to ensure
that she arrives at their destination at
exactly the same time as cyclist A?

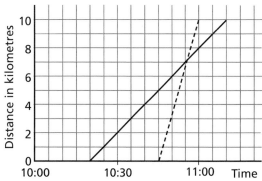

The dotted line is the distance–time graph of a car.

(c)  What is its speed in km/h?

(d)  How much further does cyclist A have to go when overtaken by the car?

(e)  When should the car have started its journey if it wanted to arrive at the destination
at exactly the same time as the cyclists?

2  The graph shows the journey of a person walking to a village shop and also a cyclist cycling to the shop and then returning.

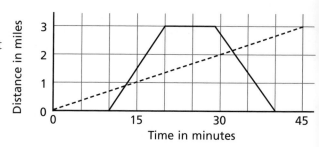

(a)  What is the difference, in m.p.h., between the speeds of the cyclist and the walker when the cyclist overtakes the walker?

(b)  Calculate, as accurately as you can, the speed of the cyclist on the return journey.

(c)  Find, as accurately as you can, how much further the cyclist has travelled than the walker between the two times when the cyclist passes the walker.

## Section C

1  Calculate the distance travelled in
   (a)  3 hours at 65 m.p.h.
   (b)  $4\frac{1}{2}$ hours at 110 km/h
   (c)  20 seconds at 12 m/s
   (d)  3 minutes at 7 m/s
   (e)  2 hours 20 minutes at 45 km/h
   (f)  25 minutes at 120 km/h

2  Calculate the time taken to travel
   (a)  140 miles at 35 m.p.h.
   (b)  750 m at 15 m/s
   (c)  240 km at 16 km per minute
   (d)  6 km at 120 m/s

3  How long, in minutes, will these journeys take?
   (a)  30 miles at 40 m.p.h.
   (b)  45 km at 75 km/h

4  Martin travelled for 15 minutes at 24 km/h then for 20 minutes at 45 km/h.
   (a)  How far did he travel?
   (b)  What was his average speed for the whole journey?

5  Traffic in London was travelling at an average speed of 3 m.p.h.
   Jody's taxi driver told her that her destination was 2 miles away.
   Jody can walk at 4 m.p.h. and the route for walking was only $1\frac{1}{2}$ miles.
   How much quicker would it be for Jody to walk, rather than stay in the taxi?

## Section D

1  Find the times taken, in hours and minutes, for these journeys.
   (a)  38 miles at 15 m.p.h.
   (b)  448 km at 105 km/h
   (c)  28 miles at 70 m.p.h.

2  Find the times for these journeys, in minutes and seconds to the nearest second.
   (a)  850 metres at 8 m/s
   (b)  1.2 km at 7 m/s
   (c)  90 cm at 1.4 m/s

**3** Find the average speed, in m.p.h. to 1 d.p., for these journeys.

    (a) 135 miles in 2 hours 25 minutes     (b) 104 miles in 1 hour 22 minutes

**4** How long, in seconds, will it take to travel 300 m at 45 km/h?

**5** These are the record times for marathon races, both achieved in 2002.
A marathon is 26 miles. Find the average speeds of these record holders.

    (a) Men's marathon: 2 hours, 5 minutes and 38 seconds

    (b) Women's marathon: 2 hours 17 minutes and 18 seconds

**6** The world record time for the men's 10 000 m race is 26 minutes 22.75 seconds.
The world junior record time for this distance is 27 minutes 11.18 seconds.

How much faster, in metres per second, was the average speed for the men's record holder than the average speed for the junior record holder?

## Section E

**1** Rohini earns £34.10 for $5\frac{1}{2}$ hours work. What is her rate of pay per hour?

**2** Matthew's typing speed is 65 words per minute. How many hours, to the nearest half hour, will it take him to type up a 25 000 word thesis?

**3** A researcher finds that, when hovering, a hummingbird completes 100 wingbeats in 1.3 seconds. What rate is this, in wingbeats per second?

**4** (a) A cog in a machine rotates once in 7.5 seconds.
       At what speed is it rotating in revolutions per minute?

    (b) Another cog rotates at the rate of 0.8 revolutions per second.
       How long will it take to complete 1000 revolutions?

**5** The world record for the number of stamps licked and stuck on to envelopes in 5 minutes is 225.

What rate is this     (a) in stamps per second         (b) in seconds per stamp

**\*6** This is a velocity–time graph for a cyclist.

    (a) What is the acceleration of the cyclist?

    (b) For how long does the cyclist travel at constant speed?

    (c) The cyclist decelerates (slows down) until she stops. At what rate does she decelerate?

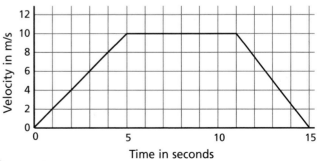

# 7 Distributions and averages

## Section A

1 The number of people in cars that passed a set of traffic lights was recorded. The data recorded is shown in the table below.

| Number of people in car | Number of cars |
|---|---|
| 1 | 10 |
| 2 | 15 |
| 3 | 12 |
| 4 | 6 |
| 5 | 7 |
| 6 | 5 |

(a) How many cars were surveyed?

(b) How many people were there altogether in the cars?

(c) Calculate the mean number of people per car.

2 The weight of eggs laid by a hen over a period of four weeks is shown in the table. Calculate the mean weight of the eggs.

| Weight | 58 g | 59 g | 60 g | 61 g | 62 g | 63 g |
|---|---|---|---|---|---|---|
| Number of eggs | 3 | 7 | 11 | 9 | 8 | 2 |

3 Here are the test results for class 10M arranged in a stem-and-leaf table. Find

(a) the median mark

(b) the range of marks

(c) the modal mark

Marks out of 20

```
0 | 8 8 9 9 9 9
1 | 0 1 1 2 5 5 6 7 8 8 9 9 9
2 | 0 0 0 0 0 0
```

4 (a) Make a stem-and-leaf table for this set of examination marks.

(b) Find the median mark and the range of the marks.

| Marks out of 60 | 19 | 25 | 38 | 48 | 39 | 56 | 42 |
|---|---|---|---|---|---|---|---|
| | 30 | 32 | 39 | 42 | 59 | 28 | 27 |
| | 57 | 45 | 44 | 42 | 37 | 28 | 18 |
| | 55 | 51 | 48 | 36 | 18 | 21 | 24 |

5 The number of letters delivered to the houses in a particular street is given in the following table. Calculate an estimate of the mean number of letters delivered to each house.

| Number of letters | Number of houses |
|---|---|
| 0–3 | 12 |
| 4–7 | 8 |
| 8–11 | 4 |
| 12–15 | 2 |

*6 In a darts match a record is kept of the scores for each throw.

| Score | 1–20 | 21–40 | 41–60 | 61–100 | 101–140 | 141–180 |
|---|---|---|---|---|---|---|
| Frequency | 5 | 20 | 37 | 62 | 6 | 3 |

Calculate an estimate of the mean score.

# Section B

1 The armspans of students in classes 10M and 9P are measured.
The results are displayed in this table.

(a) On the same axes draw frequency polygons for the armspans for 10M and 9P.

(b) Calculate estimates for the mean armspan for each class.

(c) Write a couple of sentences comparing the armspans of 10M and 9P.

| Armspan ($a$ cm) | Frequency 10M | Frequency 9P |
|---|---|---|
| $150 < a \le 155$ | 3 | 4 |
| $155 < a \le 160$ | 5 | 7 |
| $160 < a \le 165$ | 7 | 10 |
| $165 < a \le 170$ | 8 | 6 |
| $170 < a \le 175$ | 6 | 3 |
| $175 < a \le 180$ | 1 | 0 |

2 For her geography project Nina collects data about the weekly rainfall ($d$) in millimetres for her home town.
She displays the results in a table.

Calculate an estimate for the mean weekly rainfall.

| Weekly rainfall ($d$) in mm | Number of weeks |
|---|---|
| $0 < d \le 10$ | 18 |
| $10 < d \le 20$ | 20 |
| $20 < d \le 30$ | 3 |
| $30 < d \le 40$ | 4 |
| $40 < d \le 50$ | 3 |
| $50 < d \le 60$ | 4 |

# Section C

1 The lengths of 36 runner beans were measured and rounded to the nearest mm.
Make a frequency table for the given data.
Choose your own class intervals.

| 152 | 180 | 165 | 182 | 177 | 160 | 172 | 183 | 163 |
|---|---|---|---|---|---|---|---|---|
| 185 | 159 | 176 | 186 | 173 | 189 | 191 | 176 | 192 |
| 178 | 175 | 173 | 186 | 188 | 193 | 162 | 189 | 168 |
| 184 | 153 | 170 | 155 | 166 | 184 | 179 | 174 | 171 |

(a) Draw a frequency chart for the data.

(b) From your frequency table, calculate an estimate for the mean length of a runner bean.

(c) Calculate the mean of the actual lengths, and compare your estimate with it.

**2** The data below shows the amount of rain in millimetres that fell each day in February.

| | | | | | | |
|---|---|---|---|---|---|---|
| 3.5 | 16.4 | 6.4 | 3.7 | 14.2 | 8.9 | 22.9 |
| 2.9 | 7.8 | 13.9 | 14.2 | 4.5 | 11.6 | 15.9 |
| 18.9 | 0.1 | 6.1 | 1.4 | 3.1 | 2.5 | 5.6 |
| 2.6 | 9.4 | 4.1 | 17.9 | 19.2 | 10.7 | 7.2 |

(a) Draw a frequency chart to show this information.
You will need to choose sensible groups for the data.

(b) Calculate an estimate for the mean daily rainfall in February.

(c) Calculate the mean of the actual daily rainfall and compare the two results.

## Section D

**1** The table below shows the quarterly ice-cream sales for a small shop.

| Year | 1998 | 1998 | 1998 | 1999 | 1999 | 1999 | 1999 | 2000 |
|---|---|---|---|---|---|---|---|---|
| Quarter | 2 | 3 | 4 | 1 | 2 | 3 | 4 | 1 |
| Sales | 450 | 850 | 160 | 93 | 380 | 880 | 145 | 86 |

(a) Calculate a 4-point moving average and show it with the original data on a graph.

(b) Describe the trend.

**2** This table shows the amount spent on gas for a family of four.

| Year | 1998 | 1998 | 1998 | 1999 | 1999 | 1999 | 1999 | 2000 |
|---|---|---|---|---|---|---|---|---|
| Quarter | 2 | 3 | 4 | 1 | 2 | 3 | 4 | 1 |
| Amount | £65 | £38 | £195 | £112 | £55 | £42 | £172 | £109 |

(a) Calculate a 4-point moving average and show it with the original data on a graph.

(b) Describe the trend.

**3** The table shows the annual road accidents for a town.

| Year | 1994 | 1995 | 1996 | 1997 | 1998 | 1999 | 2000 | 2001 | 2002 |
|---|---|---|---|---|---|---|---|---|---|
| Accidents | 134 | 195 | 220 | 188 | 270 | 235 | 193 | 215 | 170 |

(a) Calculate a 5-point moving average and show it with the original data on a graph.

(b) Describe the trend.

# 8 Changing the subject 1

## Section B

**1** This tiling pattern has the formula $g = 2w + 6$.

(a) Rearrange the formula to make $w$ the subject.

(b) What is the value of $w$ when $g = 60$?

(c) What is the value of $w$ when $g = 96$?

(d) Check that the values of $g$ and $w$ in parts (b) and (c) fit the original formula.

**2** Rearrange each of these formulas to make the bold letter the subject.

(a) $a = 3\mathbf{b} + 7$         (b) $f = 8\mathbf{g} - 6$         (c) $r = 12 + 2\mathbf{s}$

**3** (a) Make $z$ the subject of the formula $y = 16 - 9z$.

(b) Find $z$ when $y = 52$.         (c) Find $z$ when $y = {}^-29$.

**4** Which of the following are correct rearrangements of $t = 6s - 4$?
(*s* need not be the subject of the rearrangement.)

**A** $\dfrac{t + 4}{6} = s$     **B** $t = 2(3s - 2)$     **C** $t = 3(2s - 2)$     **D** $t + s = 5s - 4$

**E** $\dfrac{4 - t}{6} = s$     **F** $6s - t = 4$

**5** (a) Copy and complete this working to make $y$ the subject of the formula $7x - 3y = 50$.

(b) Use suitable values of $x$ and $y$ to check that your rearrangement is correct.

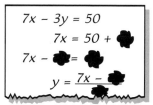

**6** Rearrange each of these formulas to make the bold letter the subject.

(a) $a + \mathbf{b} = 14$         (b) $g = 4 - 2\mathbf{h}$         (c) $5\mathbf{x} + 3y = 20$

(d) $p = 2\mathbf{q} - 18$         (e) $c = 3\mathbf{d} + 7$         (f) $r = 19 + 3\mathbf{s}$

(g) $5u = 7\mathbf{v} - 15$         (h) $8m = 3\mathbf{n} - 15$         (i) $2d - 3\mathbf{e} = 12$

## Section C

1 The formula $s = p + 2r$ connects $s$, $p$ and $r$.

  (a) Rearrange the formula to make $r$ the subject.

  (b) What is the value of $r$ when $s = 8$ and $p = 2$?

  (c) Check that this value of $r$, and the values of $s$ and $p$, fit in the original formula.

2 Copy and complete this working to make $h$ the subject of the formula $j = ah - b$.

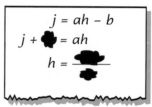

3 Rearrange each of these formulas to make the bold letter the subject.

  (a) $m = k\mathbf{n} + 2$        (b) $r = m\mathbf{y} - g$        (c) $bu = 4\mathbf{v} - w$

4 (a) Copy and complete this working to give $y$ in terms of $m$, $x$, $r$ and $n$.

  (b) Use your new formula to find $y$ when $r = 22$, $m = 5$, $x = 2$ and $n = 4$.

  (c) Use the value of $y$ you found in (b) to check that your rearrangement is correct.

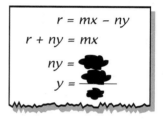

5 Which of these are correct rearrangements of $pn = g - am$?

**A**   $p = \dfrac{g - am}{n}$     **B**   $m = \dfrac{pn - g}{a}$     **C**   $m = \dfrac{g - pn}{a}$     **D**   $am = g - pn$     **E**   $am = pn + g$     **F**   $g = am - pn$

6 A household gas bill is calculated using the formula
$$C = sd + nu$$
$C$ is the total cost in **pence**;
$s$ is the standing charge in pence per day;
$d$ is the number of days;
$n$ is the number of units of gas used;
$u$ is the cost of gas in pence per unit.

  (a) Rearrange the formula to give $n$ in terms of the other variables.

  (b) How many units of gas have been charged for, if the total cost of the bill is £80.94 for a period of 90 days? The standing charge is 10p per day and the cost per unit is 1.1p.

7 Rearrange each of these formulas to make the bold letter the subject.

  (a) $pq - z = \mathbf{l}$        (b) $f = u - T\mathbf{s}$        (c) $h = u + p\mathbf{v}$

  (d) $x_1 = k\mathbf{x_0} - u$        (e) $am + b\mathbf{n} = 5$        (f) $2cd + \mathbf{w}v = r$

  (g) $P_1 = sp_2 - g\mathbf{m}$        (h) $qy = 3\mathbf{a}x - rt$

## Section D

1 (a) Copy and complete this working to give
 $s$ in terms of $r$ and $p$.

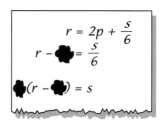

$$r = 2p + \frac{s}{6}$$
$$r - \clubsuit = \frac{s}{6}$$
$$\clubsuit(r - \clubsuit) = s$$

 (b) Find some values of $r$, $p$ and $s$ that fit the
 original formula.
 Check that they fit your rearrangement.

2 Rearrange each of these formulas to make the bold letter the subject.

 (a) $b = 3c + \dfrac{\boldsymbol{d}}{4}$        (b) $m = 4 + \dfrac{\boldsymbol{n}}{a}$        (c) $y = 2x - \dfrac{\boldsymbol{z}}{t}$

3 (a) Copy and complete this working to make
 $t$ the subject of the formula,
 where $s$ is the constant speed in m.p.h.,
 $d$ is the distance travelled in miles
 and $t$ is the time in hours.

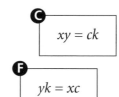

$$s = \frac{d}{t}$$
$$st = \clubsuit$$
$$t = \clubsuit$$

 (b) Find the time taken for a car travelling at
 a constant 56 m.p.h. to travel 266 miles.
 Give your answer in hours and minutes.

4 The volume of a rectangular pyramid is given by $V = \dfrac{abh}{3}$.

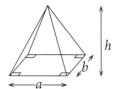

 (a) Rearrange the formula to make $h$ the subject.

 (b) Calculate the height of a rectangular pyramid
 of volume 96 cm$^3$, where $a = 4$ cm and $b = 6$ cm.

5 Here are eight formulas.
 Find the four pairs of equivalent formulas.

**A** $\quad yk = \dfrac{x}{c}$

**B** $\quad y = \dfrac{xc}{k}$

**C** $\quad xy = ck$

**D** $\quad yc = \dfrac{x}{k}$

**E** $\quad x = \dfrac{cy}{k}$

**F** $\quad yk = xc$

**G** $\quad \dfrac{y}{x} = \dfrac{k}{c}$

**H** $\quad x = \dfrac{ck}{y}$

6 The power, in watts, dissipated in an electric circuit is given by $W = I^2R$.
 $I$ stands for the current in amps,
 $R$ is the resistance of the circuit in ohms.

 (a) Rearrange the formula to give $I$ in terms of $W$ and $R$.

 (b) Calculate the current in an electric circuit where $W = 150$ watts
 and $R = 12.25$ ohms.

7 Make the bold letter the subject of each of these.

(a) $k = \frac{1}{2}mv^2$      (b) $k = \frac{1}{2}\mathbf{m}v^2$      (c) $M = \frac{p\mathbf{l}^2}{12}$      (d) $M = \frac{\mathbf{p}l^2}{12}$

8 Make $l$ the subject of the formula $T = 2\pi\sqrt{\dfrac{l}{g}}$

9 The volume of an Easter egg is given by $V = \dfrac{2\pi r^2 h}{3}$.
$r$ is the radius shown and $h$ is the height, both in cm.

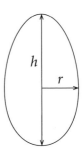

(a) Rearrange this formula to make $r$ the subject.

(b) Work out the radius of an Easter egg whose height is 16 cm and volume is 850 cm³.
Give your answer to an appropriate degree of accuracy.

10 Copy and complete this working to make $p$ the subject of this formula.

Check your rearrangement is correct by substituting values in the original and your rearrangement.

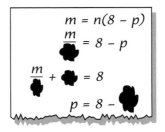

$m = n(8 - p)$

$\dfrac{m}{\phantom{n}} = 8 - p$

$\dfrac{m}{\phantom{n}} + \phantom{n} = 8$

$p = 8 - \phantom{n}$

11 Write each formula in terms of the bold letter.

(a) $c = 16(\mathbf{d} + e)$      (b) $r = m(y - \mathbf{x})$      (c) $j = l + \dfrac{k}{h}$

12 The extended length of a material with a force applied is given by the formula

$$l = l_0\left(1 + \frac{F}{AE}\right)$$

$l$ stands for the extended length in mm;
$l_0$ stands for the original length in mm;
$F$ stands for the applied force in newtons (N);
$A$ stands for the cross-sectional area in mm²;
$E$ stands for Young's modulus in N/mm².

(a) Rearrange the formula to give $F$ in terms of $l$, $l_0$, $A$ and $E$.

(b) What force needs to be applied to a piece of nylon fishing line, cross-sectional area 0.2 mm², to extend its length from 1000 mm to 1005 mm?
(Young's modulus $E = 2500$ N/mm² for nylon.)

# 9 Increase and decrease

## Section A

1 Write down the decimal equivalent of

   (a) 46%    (b) 8%    (c) 35.2%   (d) 112%   (e) 7.5%   (f) 137.5%

2 It rained on 13 days during March.
   What percentage of the days in March were rainy?

3 In a box of 24 pencils, 7 need sharpening.
   What percentage (to the nearest 0.1%) of the pencils in the box need sharpening?

4 (a) To increase 85 by 12% you must multiply 85 by…?
   (b) Increase 85 by 12%.

5 (a) To decrease 69 by 71% you multiply 69 by…?
   (b) Decrease 69 by 71%.

6 (a) Increase £125 by 18%.          (b) Decrease £150 by 22%.
   (c) Increase £40 by 120%.

7 A shop reduces prices by 12% in a sale.
   What is the sale price of a coat costing £135?

8 A firm is going to give its workers a 5% pay rise.
   What will be the new rate of pay of a worker earning £8.60 per hour?

9 A car costing £15 000 when new was sold for £11 400 when it was one year old.
   What was the percentage decrease in value?

10 Two years ago a house was worth £150 000.
   During the first year its value increased by 8%.
   During the second year its value decreased by 1%.

   What is its value now?

11 A 330 ml can of drink costs 52p.

   The can is to be replaced by a 500 ml can costing 69p. Calculate

   (a) the percentage increase in the size
   (b) the percentage increase in the cost
   (c) the percentage change in the cost per litre

## Section B

**1** This diagram represents a 10% increase followed by another 10% increase.

(a) Calculate the overall percentage change.

Calculate the overall percentage changes represented by these diagrams.

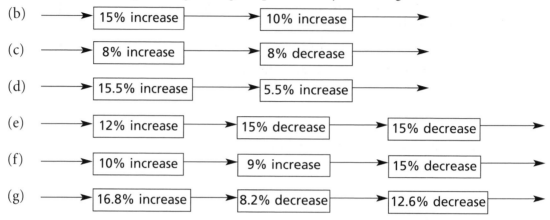

(b) 15% increase → 10% increase

(c) 8% increase → 8% decrease

(d) 15.5% increase → 5.5% increase

(e) 12% increase → 15% decrease → 15% decrease

(f) 10% increase → 9% increase → 15% decrease

(g) 16.8% increase → 8.2% decrease → 12.6% decrease

**2** A firm gave its workers a 4% pay rise last year and a 3.8% pay rise this year.
Calculate the percentage pay rise over the two years to the nearest 0.1%.

**3** Over the past three years, the volume of water in a pond has
decreased by 10% each year.
What is the overall percentage decrease over the three years?

**4** In January a garage reduced the price of a car by 8%.
In February the garage reduced the price of the car by a further 7%.
What was the overall percentage decrease in price?

**5** Last year a travel agent increased the price of a holiday to Spain by 8%.
This year they decreased the price by 5%.
What was the overall percentage increase in price?

**6** The population of a town decreased by 3.8% in 1996.
The population increased by 3% in 1997.
What was the overall percentage change in population?

**7** Over two years the average attendance at a football ground increased by 26%.
The attendance increased by 15% in the first year.
What was the percentage increase during the second year?

## Section C

1 £650 is put into a bank account which pays interest at the rate of 8% per annum.

Copy and complete this table showing the amount in the account at the end of each year.
(Round your answers to the nearest penny.)

| Years | Amount |
|-------|--------|
| 0 | £650.00 |
| 1 | £702.00 |
| 2 | |
| 3 | |
| 4 | |

2 Stephen invested £700 in a building society account that was paying 4.5% p.a. interest. How much did he have in his account after

(a) 1 year       (b) 2 years       (c) 3 years       (d) 4 years

(Round your answers to the nearest penny.)

3 Which final amount is larger?

(a) £500 invested for 3 years at 4% p.a.

(b) £500 invested for 4 years at 3% p.a.

4 Calculate the final amount, to the nearest penny, when

(a) £750 is invested at 5% p.a. for 8 years

(b) £850 is invested at 3.75% p.a. for 12 years

5 £2000 is invested in an account which pays interest at 6% per annum. How many years will it have to stay in the account before it is worth £3000?

6 The value of a painting increases by 4% each year. If it is worth £350 now, how much will it be worth in 10 years time?

7 The number of people attending a cinema decreases by 6% every year. What is the overall percentage decrease in attendances over 3 years?

8 A bank charges interest on a loan at a rate of 1.8% per month. Calculate the overall percentage rate per year, giving your answer to the nearest 0.1%.

9 Samantha opens a new bank account with £1000. The account pays 5.2% p.a. interest. She pays an extra £1000 into the account at the end of each year.

How much will there be in Samantha's account when

(a) her first extra payment is due

(b) her second extra payment is due

(c) her fourth extra payment is due

## Section D

1 The population of a town increased by 5% during the last ten years.
The present population is 16 000.
What was the population ten years ago?
(Round your answer to the nearest 100.)

2 A television costs £399.
This price includes VAT at 17.5%.
What is the cost of the television before VAT is added?

3 A shop reduced the price of shoes by 25% in a sale.
A pair of shoes cost £24 in the sale.
What was the price of the pair of shoes before it was reduced for the sale?

4 A restaurant includes a service charge of 12% which is added to the bill.
A customer in the restaurant paid £19.60, including service charge, for a meal.
What was the price of the meal before the service charge was added?

5 The cost of a drawing program was reduced by 10% to £89.99.
What was the cost of the software before the reduction?

6 The price of a radio was increased by 5%.
If the new price of the radio is £38, what was the increase in price?

7 The number of viewers watching a weekly television programme
increased by 15% when an episode showed the two stars getting married.
5.4 million watched the wedding episode.

How many more people watched the wedding episode than the episode
the previous week? (Give your answer correct to three significant figures.)

8 A dress which should have been dry-cleaned shrank by 6% when
it was washed by mistake.
The length of the dress after it had shrunk was 105 cm.
How many centimetres did the dress shrink?

9 A magazine's sales figures have dropped by 12% in the past year to 32 478.
How many more copies did the magazine sell last year?

## Section E

1 Andrea's annual salary for the past year has been £25 650.
  She will get a pay increase for the next year equal to the
  annual rate of inflation, which is 2.4%.
  Calculate her new salary.

2 The number of squirrels in a wood has increased from 242 to 248 in the past year.

  (a) Calculate the percentage increase in the number of squirrels.

  (b) If the number of squirrels continues to increase at the same rate each year,
      how many squirrels will there be in the wood in five years' time?

3 A garage owner reduced the selling price of a car from £6299 to £5999.

  (a) What was the percentage reduction in price?

  He still could not sell the car so he reduced its price by a further 7.5%.

  (b) What was the final selling price (to the nearest £)?

  (c) Calculate the overall percentage decrease in price.

4 The owners of a toll bridge increase the toll for cars crossing the bridge by 8%.
  As a consequence, 5% of the drivers who used the bridge decided
  to use an alternative route.
  Calculate the percentage change in toll money taken.

5 John increased the area of his lawn by 11% to 204 m$^2$.
  What was the original area of the lawn?

6 April 1998 was a particularly wet month with 124.9 mm of rain falling
  on average across the UK.
  This rainfall was 102% higher than the normal average rainfall for April.

  (a) What is the normal average rainfall for April across the UK?

  (b) How much more rain than normal fell in April 1998?

7 One month a shop sold 84 DVD players.
  The shop then increased its sales of DVD players by 150% in the next month.
  How many DVD players did it sell in the second month?

8 In one year the number of shops selling mobile phones in a city increased
  from 15 to 78.
  What was the percentage increase?

9 One year the value of an investment increased by 3%.
  The following year the value of the investment decreased by 7%.
  What was the percentage decrease in the value of the investment over the two years?

# Mixed questions 2

1 Rearrange each of these formulas to make the bold letter the subject.

  (a) $b = 4(\boldsymbol{a} - 1)$     (b) $q = \dfrac{3\boldsymbol{p} - 1}{2}$     (c) $d = 5 - 3\boldsymbol{c}$     (d) $t = 8 + \dfrac{\boldsymbol{s}}{2}$

2 The population of a town is planned to increase by 15% over the next three years and by 10% over the three years after that.

  The present population is 10 000. Calculate, to the nearest hundred, the planned population in six years' time.

3 This table shows the distribution of the weights of some young children.

  Calculate an estimate of the mean weight of the children.

| Weight, $w$ kg | Frequency |
|---|---|
| $3.0 < w \le 3.5$ | 8 |
| $3.5 < w \le 4.0$ | 14 |
| $4.0 < w \le 4.5$ | 11 |
| $4.5 < w \le 5.0$ | 7 |

4 Calculate length CD in this diagram.

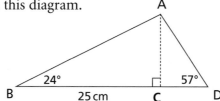

⊠ 5 A small pump can empty a pool in twenty minutes working at a rate of 450 litres per minute.
   A large pump could empty the same pool in 12 minutes.
   How long would it take to empty the pool if both pumps worked together?

6 Rearrange each of these formulas to make the bold letter the subject.

  (a) $y = a\boldsymbol{x}^2 + b$     (b) $y = ax - \boldsymbol{b}$     (c) $w = \dfrac{\sqrt{\boldsymbol{u} - st}}{n}$     (d) $t = p + \dfrac{qs^2}{\boldsymbol{r}}$

7 Marji opens a building society account with £200.
   The building society pays interest at a rate of 5.5% a year.

   How many full years will Marji have to leave the money in the account for it to grow to at least £250?

8 Calculate length QR in this diagram.

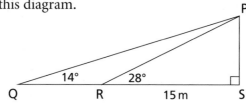

# 10 *Using area and volume*

## *Sections A and B*

1 Calculate the areas of
these parallelograms.

(a)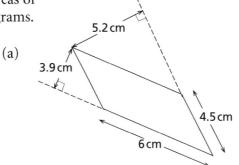

(b)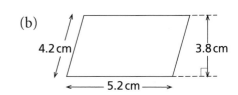

2 Find the missing lengths in
each of these parallelograms.

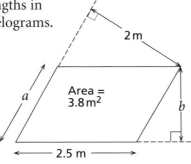

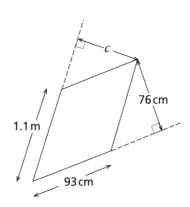

3 The area of each of these three
parallelograms is $76.8\,\text{cm}^2$.
Find the missing lengths.

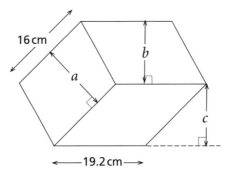

4 These triangles have equal areas.
Find the missing lengths.

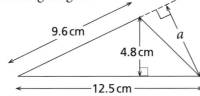

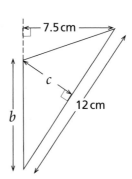

**5** For parts (a) and (b) find, and simplify, an expression for the shaded area.

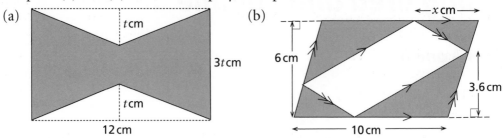

(a) $t$ cm, $3t$ cm, $t$ cm, 12 cm

(b) $x$ cm, 6 cm, 3.6 cm, 10 cm

(c) In both parts (a) and (b) the shaded area is $30\,\text{cm}^2$.

(i) Form and solve an equation to find the value of $t$.

(ii) Form and solve an equation to find the value of $x$.

## Section C

**1** Find the area of these trapeziums in (i) $\text{mm}^2$ (ii) $\text{cm}^2$.

(a) 7 mm, 12 mm, 8 mm, 15 mm

(b) 3.4 cm, 2.4 cm, 12 mm

**2** Find the missing lengths in these trapeziums.

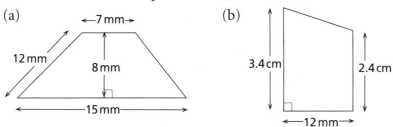

5.4 cm, 5.4 cm, Area = 32.39 cm², $a$, 4.1 cm

3.3 cm, Area = 8.6 cm², $b$, 5.3 cm

## Section D

**1** (a) France has an area of $551\,500\,\text{km}^2$ and its population is $58\,886\,000$.
Calculate the population density of France.

(b) The area of Germany is $357\,000\,\text{km}^2$ and the population density is 230 per $\text{km}^2$.
Estimate the population of Germany.

**2** This table shows typical yields from some vegetables.

(a) What weight of potatoes should you get from a plot with area 20.5 m² ?

(b) What weight of broad beans should you get from a rectangular plot 4.2 m by 1.5 m?

(c) How many cucumbers should you get from a rectangular plot 2.5 m by 0.5 m?

| Vegetable | Yield |
|-----------|-------|
| Aubergine | 5.0 kg/m² |
| Broad bean | 3.8 kg/m² |
| French bean | 2.5 kg/m² |
| Cucumber | 16 cucumbers/m² |
| Potato | 4.0 kg/m² |

(d) What area is needed to get 22 kg of broad beans (to the nearest 0.1 m²)?

(e) A gardener has a plot with area 6.5 m².
He wants to fill it, growing aubergines and French beans only.
He wants the weight of French beans he grows to be twice the weight of aubergines.
What area should he give to each crop and what weights would he expect to get?

## Section E

**1** For this prism calculate

(a) its volume

(b) its surface area

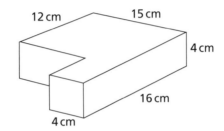

**2** A fruit drink dispenser is in the shape of a cuboid measuring 20 cm by 28 cm by 40 cm. How many 350 ml fruit drinks can be dispensed from a full container?

**3** The cross-section of this prism is an equilateral triangle of side 8 cm. The length of the prism is 5 cm.

(a) Use Pythagoras to calculate the height of the triangular cross-section.

(b) Calculate the volume of the prism.

(c) Calculate the surface area of the prism.

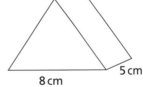

**4** (a) How many cubic metres of water are needed to fill this swimming pool?

(b) Calculate the length of the slope marked $x$.

(c) The inside of the pool is covered with white tiles. Calculate the approximate number of tiles needed if each tile measures 20 cm by 20 cm.

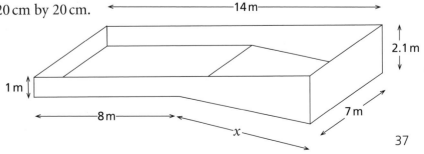

37

## Section F

**1** A set of ten cork table mats each measuring 31.5 cm by 20 cm by 4 mm has a mass of 0.605 kg.
What is the density of cork?

**2** The density of sugar is 1.59 g/cm³.
What is the volume of a kilogram bag of sugar?

**3** A statue has mass 28 kg and is made of stone with density 3.2 g/cm³.
It is immersed in water in a tank with vertical sides
and with a base measuring 85 cm by 40 cm.

By how much will the water level in the tank rise when the statue is put in?

**4** This picture shows an aluminium-framed greenhouse which is delivered as a kit including all the glass.

The glass is 3 mm thick horticultural grade glass with a density of 2.4 g/cm³.

What is the mass of the glass?
(Ignore space taken up by the aluminium frame.)

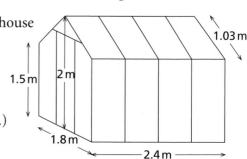

## Section G

**1** A tablecloth measures 150 cm by 240 cm.
   (a) Calculate the area of the cloth in cm².   (b) Convert your answer to m².

**2** A piece of paper measures 0.6 m by 0.45 m.
   (a) Calculate the area of the paper in m².   (b) Convert your answer to cm².

**3** A credit card measures 8.5 cm by 5.4 cm.
   (a) Calculate the area of the card in cm².   (b) Convert your answer to mm².

**4** A farm has an area of 450 hectares.
   What area is this in      (a) m²      (b) km²

**5** (a) The surface area of a box is 5250 mm². What is this area in cm²?
   (b) The volume of the box is 12.8 cm³. What is this volume in mm³?

**6** A bucket can be filled with 12 000 cm³ of sand.
   How many buckets of sand can you get from 1 cubic metre of sand?

**7** An oil tank has volume 2.5 m³.
   How many 5 litre containers of oil can be filled from the tank?

# 11 Sine and cosine

## Section A

**1** Find the missing angles and lengths.

(a)
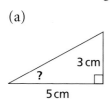

(b)
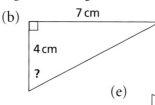
7 cm
4 cm
?

(c)
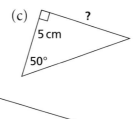
5 cm
50°
?

(d)
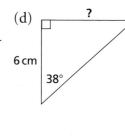
6 cm
38°
?

(e)
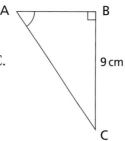
2 cm
?
7.8 cm

**2** In a triangle ABC, tan A = 0.25.

(a) What is the length of AB?

(b) Use Pythagoras to find the length AC.

A     B

9 cm

C

**3** Find the missing lengths.

(a)
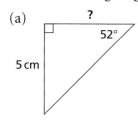
?
52°
5 cm

(b)
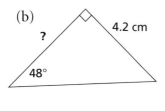
?
4.2 cm
48°

(c)
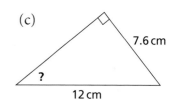
?
71°
3.2 cm

(d)
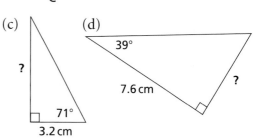
39°
7.6 cm
?

## Sections B, C and D

**1** Find the missing angles in these right-angled triangles.

(a)
?
13 cm
40 cm

(b)
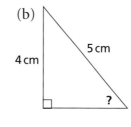
5 cm
4 cm
?

(c)
7.6 cm
?
12 cm

(d)
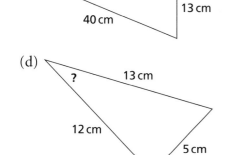
?
13 cm
12 cm
5 cm

(e)
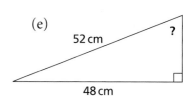
52 cm
?
48 cm

39

**2** Find the missing lengths.

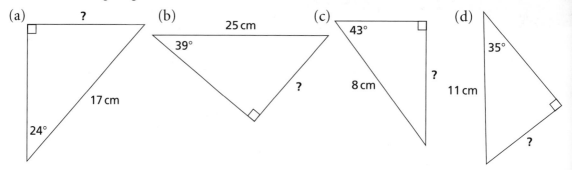

(a) ?  17 cm  24°

(b) 25 cm  39°

(c) 43°  8 cm  ?

(d) 35°  11 cm  ?

**3** Find the missing lengths.

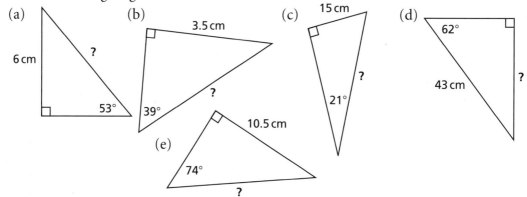

(a) 6 cm  ?  53°

(b) 3.5 cm  ?  39°

(c) 15 cm  ?  21°

(d) 62°  43 cm  ?

(e) 10.5 cm  74°  ?

## Section E

**1** Copy and complete these diagrams and statements.

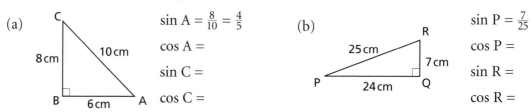

(a) C  10 cm  8 cm  B  6 cm  A

$\sin A = \frac{8}{10} = \frac{4}{5}$

$\cos A =$

$\sin C =$

$\cos C =$

(b) R  25 cm  7 cm  P  24 cm  Q

$\sin P = \frac{7}{25}$

$\cos P =$

$\sin R =$

$\cos R =$

**2** Find the missing angles.

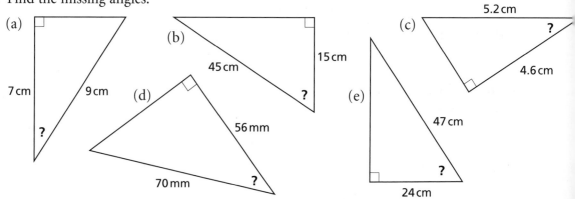

(a) 7 cm  9 cm  ?

(b) 45 cm  15 cm  ?

(c) 5.2 cm  ?  4.6 cm

(d) 56 mm  70 mm  ?

(e) 47 cm  24 cm  ?

**3** (a) If $\cos A = \frac{3}{4}$, what is angle A?  (b) If $\cos A = 0.5$, what is angle A?

**4** Find the missing lengths in these right-angled triangles.

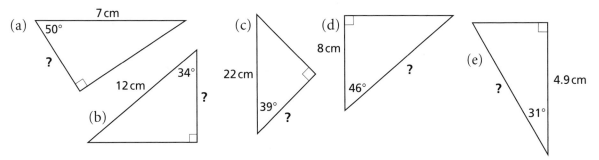

## Section F

**1** Find the angles or lengths marked $x$ in each triangle.

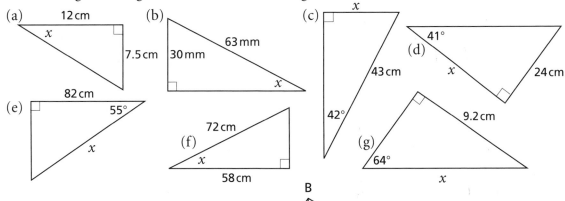

**2** ABCD is a design for a children's slide. BD is 136 cm, DC is 195 cm.

(a) Calculate angle BCD.

(b) Angle ABD is 28°. Calculate distance AB.

**3** The angle of elevation of a kite is shown from two positions, Q and R. PQ = 70 m.

(a) Calculate the height of the kite PS.

(b) Calculate the length RS.

**4** The height of a yacht's mast BE is 8 m. Calculate length AD.

# 12 *Large and little*

## Sections A and B

1  A car owner drives an average of 20 miles every day.
At this rate, how many years would it take her to
drive a million miles?

2  A quadrillion is $10^{15}$.
Write this number out in full.

3  Iceland has an area of 103 000 sq km.
Which of the following are ways to write its area?

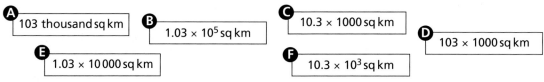

**A** 103 thousand sq km
**B** $1.03 \times 10^5$ sq km
**C** $10.3 \times 1000$ sq km
**D** $103 \times 1000$ sq km
**E** $1.03 \times 10\,000$ sq km
**F** $10.3 \times 10^3$ sq km

4  If you take 13 cards at random from a shuffled pack of playing cards, the chance
that they are all the same suit (e.g. all clubs) is approximately 1 in $1.6 \times 10^{11}$.
How many billion is $1.6 \times 10^{11}$?

5  Satellite data and ground rainfall measurements were used to study
variations in the size of the Sahara Desert from 1980 to 1997.
The area of the Sahara Desert varied from 9 980 000 km$^2$ in 1984 to
8 600 000 km$^2$ in 1994 and had an average area of 9 150 000 km$^2$.

(a) (i)  Write the maximum, minimum and average areas of the Sahara Desert between
1980 and 1997 in millions of km$^2$.

(ii)  What is the difference between the maximum and minimum area?

(b)  About $5 \times 10^7$ km$^2$ of the Earth's land surface is desert.
How many million km$^2$ are desert?

6  The table shows the areas of the seven
largest oceans and seas.

(a)  Copy the table, writing the areas in
millions to the nearest million km$^2$.

(b)  The total area of sea is about
360 million km$^2$.
What percentage of the sea is taken
up by the Pacific Ocean?

| | |
|---|---|
| Pacific Ocean | 166 242 000 km$^2$ |
| Atlantic Ocean | 86 557 000 km$^2$ |
| Indian Ocean | 73 427 500 km$^2$ |
| Arctic Ocean | 13 224 000 km$^2$ |
| South China Sea | 2 975 000 km$^2$ |
| Caribbean Sea | 2 516 000 km$^2$ |
| Mediterranean Sea | 2 510 000 km$^2$ |

## Section C

1 Write these numbers in standard form.

(a) 4 000 000      (b) 28 000      (c) 603 000

(d) 10 000 000      (e) 416 000      (f) 32 000 000 000

2 Write these numbers in ordinary form.

(a) $3 \times 10^5$      (b) $1 \times 10^8$      (c) $3.2 \times 10^4$

(d) $6.3 \times 10^3$      (e) $2.86 \times 10^4$      (f) $6.13 \times 10^9$

3 Write these numbers in standard form.

(a) $35 \times 10^3$      (b) $627 \times 10^4$      (c) $300 \times 10^5$      (d) $0.8 \times 10^4$

4 Between 1947 and 1980, 450 000 people died in earthquakes.
Write the number of people who died in earthquakes in standard form.

5 The table shows the attendance figures for the first
six years of the Premier Football League
(to the nearest 100 000).

(a) Rewrite the table, giving the
attendances in standard form.

In 1998–9, the total attendance figure for the
Premier League and Divisions 1 to 3 was
25.4 million people.

(b) Write this number in standard form.

| Year | Attendance |
|---|---|
| 1992–3 | 9 800 000 |
| 1993–4 | 10 600 000 |
| 1994–5 | 11 200 000 |
| 1995–6 | 10 500 000 |
| 1996–7 | 10 800 000 |
| 1997–8 | 11 100 000 |

6 The circumference of the Earth is approximately $4 \times 10^7$ m.
Write this distance as an ordinary number.

7 The average distance of the Moon from the Earth is $3.844 \times 10^5$ km.
Write this in ordinary form.

## Section D

The information shows the population (1999) and the area of different countries.

| Country | Population | Area (km$^2$) |
|---|---|---|
| Brazil | $2.7 \times 10^8$ | $8.4 \times 10^6$ |
| China | $1.3 \times 10^9$ | $9.9 \times 10^6$ |
| India | $1.0 \times 10^9$ | $3.1 \times 10^6$ |
| Russia | $1.5 \times 10^8$ | $1.7 \times 10^7$ |
| South Africa | $4.3 \times 10^7$ | $1.2 \times 10^6$ |
| United Kingdom | $5.9 \times 10^7$ | $2.4 \times 10^5$ |
| United States | $2.7 \times 10^8$ | $9.1 \times 10^6$ |

1 (a) Which of these countries has the smallest area?

  (b) Does the largest country have the largest population?
   Explain your answer.

  (c) Does the smallest country have the smallest population?
   Explain your answer.

2 Copy and complete the following statements.

  (a) The area of China is about ............ times the area of South Africa.

  (b) ........... more people live in Brazil than Russia.

  (c) The area of the United States is about ............ times the area of the United Kingdom.

  (d) The population of India is about ............... times the population of Brazil.

  (e) China is .............. km$^2$ bigger than India.

  (f) Russia is .............. km$^2$ bigger than the United States.

3 The population density of a country is the number of people who live in each square kilometre.

$$\text{population density} = \frac{\text{population}}{\text{area}}$$

  (a) Calculate the population density of each of the seven countries, giving your answers correct to one significant figure.

  (b) Arrange the countries in order of population density, highest first.

## Section E

1 Write these numbers in ordinary form.

   (a) $1 \times 10^{-2}$                (b) $2.3 \times 10^{-4}$           (c) $3.8 \times 10^{-6}$

   (d) $5.1 \times 10^{-4}$             (e) $2.6 \times 10^{-12}$         (f) $8.08 \times 10^{-7}$

2 Write these numbers in standard form.

   (a) $0.000003$              (b) $0.00000672$         (c) $0.000569$

   (d) $0.000000001$          (e) $0.0003008$          (f) $0.0000000000004$

3 If you take four cards from a pack of playing cards, the probability that they are all aces is $0.00000369$ (correct to 3 s.f.).

   (a) Which of these are ways of writing this probability?

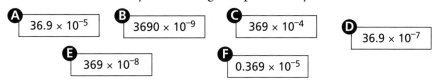

A $\quad 36.9 \times 10^{-5}$    B $\quad 3690 \times 10^{-9}$    C $\quad 369 \times 10^{-4}$    D $\quad 36.9 \times 10^{-7}$

E $\quad 369 \times 10^{-8}$    F $\quad 0.369 \times 10^{-5}$

   (b) Write the probability in standard form.

4 A nanosecond is $0.000000001$ seconds.
   Write this number in standard form.

5 A scruple was an old measure used by apothecaries.
   One scruple weighed about $1.3 \times 10^{-4}\,\text{kg}$ .
   Write this number in ordinary form.

6 The probability of rolling six consecutive sixes when rolling a standard dice six times is $2.14 \times 10^{-5}$ (correct to 3 s.f.)
   Write this probability in ordinary form.

7 A honeybee uses up $8 \times 10^{-4}$ joules of energy for every wingbeat.
   Work out how much energy is used for 50 wingbeats and write the answer in

   (a) standard form                 (b) ordinary form

8 The lightest recorded insect is a parasitic wasp which weighs $5 \times 10^{-9}\,\text{kg}$.
   Write this weight in ordinary form.

## Section F

1 Write the answers to these calculations to two significant figures in standard form.

   (a) $(4.8 \times 10^{-6}) \times (4.6 \times 10^{-7})$     (b) $(1.6 \times 10^{-4}) \times (3.8 \times 10^3)$

   (c) $\dfrac{6.7 \times 10^{-6}}{5.7 \times 10^7}$     (d) $\dfrac{8 \times 10^3}{1.03 \times 10^{-5}}$

2 Write the answers to these calculations in ordinary form, giving your answers correct to two significant figures.

   (a) $(3.6 \times 10^{-2}) \times (5.2 \times 10^3)$     (b) $(5.1 \times 10^6) \times (3.9 \times 10^{-7})$

   (c) $\dfrac{1.2 \times 10^6}{3.0 \times 10^{-7}}$     (d) $\dfrac{7.2 \times 10^{-4}}{9.8 \times 10^{-4}}$

3 An amu (atomic mass unit) is $1.660\,33 \times 10^{-27}$ kg.
   What will be the mass in kilograms of a particle with mass 15 amu?

The table shows the atomic mass of various elements measured in amus.

| Element | Atomic mass (amus) |
|---------|--------------------|
| Lead | 207.19 |
| Oxygen | 15.9994 |
| Copper | 63.546 |
| Zinc | 65.381 |
| Sulphur | 32.064 |
| Hydrogen | 1.0079 |

4 Copy and complete these statements, giving your answers correct to 3 s.f.

   (a) The mass of an atom of lead is $207.19 \times (1.66033 \times 10^{-27})$ kg $\approx$ .......... kg.

   (b) The mass of an atom of copper is about ............... kg.

   (c) An atom of zinc weighs about ............... kg more than an atom of copper.

5 A molecule of water consists of two atoms of hydrogen and one atom of oxygen.
   What is the mass, in kg, of one molecule of water (correct to 6 s.f.)?

6 A molecule of copper sulphate consists of one atom of copper,
   one atom of sulphur and four atoms of oxygen.
   What is the mass, in kg, of one molecule of copper sulphate (correct to 6 s.f.)?

## Section G

In questions 1 to 3, give your answers to the calculations in standard form.

**1** (a) $36 \times 10\,000$      (b) $0.29 \times 100\,000$      (c) $53 \times 10^6$

     (d) $0.03 \times 10^7$      (e) $71 \times 10^{-3}$      (f) $0.29 \times 10^{-4}$

**2** (a) $78 \div 1000$      (b) $106 \div 1\,000\,000$      (c) $5.9 \div 10^6$

     (d) $7.2 \div 10^{-8}$      (e) $0.38 \div 10^{-7}$      (f) $0.03 \div 10^9$

**3** (a) $\dfrac{64\,000\,000}{8000}$      (b) $\dfrac{1.2 \times 10^{11}}{3000}$      (c) $\dfrac{2.4 \times 10^8}{6 \times 10^5}$

     (d) $\dfrac{9 \times 10^4}{3 \times 10^{-6}}$      (e) $\dfrac{4.5 \times 10^{-7}}{9 \times 10^3}$      (f) $\dfrac{6 \times 10^{-5}}{1.2 \times 10^3}$

**4** Calculate the following, giving your answers in ordinary form.

     (a) $(3 \times 10^3) \times 10^5$      (b) $(2 \times 10^{-4}) \times (6 \times 10^5)$    (c) $(7 \times 10^{-9}) \times (3 \times 10^4)$

     (d) $\dfrac{3.6 \times 10^3}{10^5}$      (e) $\dfrac{4.8 \times 10^4}{1.2 \times 10^2}$      (f) $\dfrac{7 \times 10^{-5}}{1.4 \times 10^3}$

**5** Calculate the following, giving your answers in standard form.

     (a) $(3 \times 10^{-4})^2$      (b) $(5 \times 10^3)^2$      (c) $(2 \times 10^4)^3$

**6** (a) Round each of these numbers to one significant figure.

     $\boxed{A = 2.36 \times 10^8}$    $\boxed{B = 2.89 \times 10^{-7}}$    $\boxed{C = 4.7 \times 10^{-3}}$    $\boxed{D = 6.45 \times 10^{10}}$

     (b) Use your answers to work out an estimate for each of these calculations.
        Give each answer in standard form correct to one significant figure.

        (i) $A \times B$      (ii) $B \times D$      (iii) $B \times C$

        (iv) $D \div A$      (v) $B \div D$      (vi) $C \div A$

**7** (a) Write each of these numbers in standard form, to one significant figure.

     $\boxed{P = 583\,000}$    $\boxed{Q = 0.000\,795}$    $\boxed{R = 0.002\,16}$    $\boxed{S = 39\,600}$

     (b) Use your answers to work out an estimate for each of these calculations.
        Give each answer in ordinary form.

        (i) $P \times Q$    (ii) $R \times S$    (iii) $P \div S$    (iv) $R \div Q$

# 13 *Gradients and equations*

## Sections A and B

1 Find the gradient of
  each of these lines.

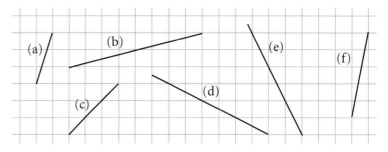

2 Find the gradients of the lines joining
  - (a) (0, 2) and (2, 4)
  - (c) (⁻2, 0) and (2, ⁻4)
  - (b) (⁻1, ⁻4) and (2, 5)
  - (d) (⁻4, 1) and (4, ⁻3)

3 Roger walks from Vendrell to the beach at Salvador and then returns to Vendrell.
  The travel graph of his journey is shown.
  Describe each stage of the journey, giving times taken and speeds.

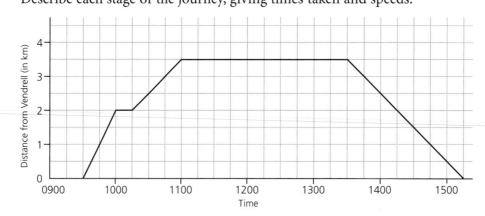

## Sections C and D

1 For each line in the diagram on the right, find
  - (i)  the gradient
  - (ii) the coordinates of the point where
    it crosses the *y*-axis
  - (iii) the equation of the line

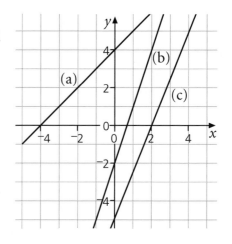

**2** A line has equation $y = 5x + 3$.
From the equation write down the gradient of the line and where it crosses the $y$-axis.

**3** A line has a gradient of $^-2$ and crosses the $y$-axis at $(0, 4)$.
Write down the equation of the line.

**4** A line passes through the points $(0, 4)$ and $(6, 4)$.
  (a) What is the gradient of the line?
  (b) Write down the equation of the line.

**5** A line passes through the points $(0, 6)$ and $(6, 0)$.
  (a) What is the gradient of the line?
  (b) Write down the equation of the line.

**6** A line has equation $y = ax + b$.
  (a) What is the gradient of the line?
  (b) What are the coordinates of the point where it crosses the $y$-axis?

**7** Calculate the gradient of each line using the scales on the axes.

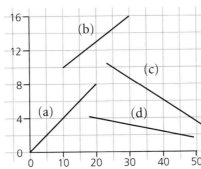
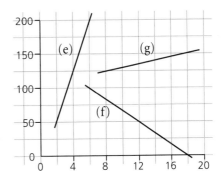

**8** Find the equation of each of these lines.

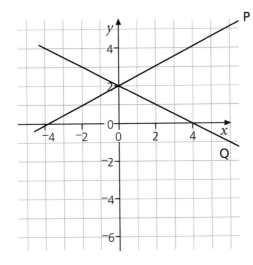
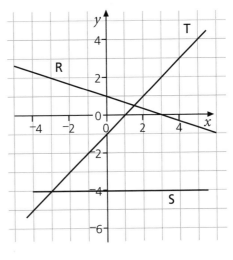

**9** A line has a gradient of $\frac{2}{5}$ and it cuts the $y$-axis at $(0, 4)$.
Write down the equation of the line.

**10** A line has equation $y = \frac{3}{4}x - 2$.

    (a) What is the gradient of the line?

    (b) What are the coordinates of the $y$-intercept?

    (c) The line passes through the point $(4, 1)$.
        Find another pair of integer coordinates that the line passes through.

## Sections E and F

**1** On squared paper draw lines with gradient

    (a) 1         (b) 2         (c) $\frac{3}{2}$         (d) $-\frac{1}{4}$

    Draw the line perpendicular to each one above and label it with its gradient.

**2** A line has gradient $\frac{4}{5}$. What is the gradient of the line perpendicular to it?

**3** A line has gradient $\frac{p}{q}$. What is the gradient of the line perpendicular to it?

**4** What is the equation of the line perpendicular to $y = 2x + 4$ that goes through $(0, {}^-2)$?

**5** Find the gradient and $y$-intercept of the lines with the following equations.

    (a) $^-3x + y = 5$         (b) $5 - x + y = 0$

    (c) $3y + 10x = 3$         (d) $4x = 2(3 - y)$

**6** Write down the equations of any three lines parallel to

    (a) $2x - 2y - 7 = 0$         (b) $2x - 3 + 4y = 0$

**7** Which of the following equations represent lines that are perpendicular to each other?

| $2y = 2x + 10$ | $2y = {}^-x + 5$ | $2y - 3x = 6$ |
| --- | --- | --- |
| $2x - 15 - 3y = 0$ | $x + y = 5$ | $2x - y = 0$ |

**8** Shape PQRS is a kite.
Angle PQR = 90°.
The line QR has equation $2y + x = 4$.

Find the equations of the lines PQ, PS and RS.

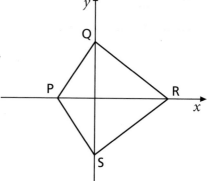

## Sections G and H

1 Find in the form $y = mx + c$ the equation of the line through
(a) $(4, 70)$ and $(7, 82)$   (b) $(27.8, 14.4)$ and $(28.3, 13.4)$
(c) $(5, 2)$ and $(13, 4)$   (d) $(^-21, 6)$ and $(14, ^-1)$

2 The coordinates of three vertices of a square PQRS are
P $(14, ^-10)$, Q $(20, 20)$ and R $(50, 14)$.
Find the equations of the lines QR, PQ and RS.

3 The lines $y = rx + 4$ and $3y = (r + 3)x - 5$ are parallel.
Find the value of $r$.

4 Television repair charges depend on the time taken for a repair.
Here are some of the charges.

| Time in minutes ($T$) | 50 | 80 | 100 | 180 |
|---|---|---|---|---|
| Charge in £ ($C$) | 35 | 50 | 60 | 100 |

(a) Sketch a graph of the charge ($C$) against the time ($T$).
(b) Find the equation that links the charge and the time in the form $C = $ .....
(c) What is the 'call-out charge' (the amount you pay even if no repair is needed)?
(d) Use your equation to work out the charge for a repair that takes $3\frac{1}{2}$ hours.

5 Sue dropped a bouncy ball from different heights.
She measured the height of the first bounce each time.
Here are her results.

| Height ball dropped from (in cm) | 30 | 50 | 80 | 100 | 120 |
|---|---|---|---|---|---|
| Height of first bounce (in cm) | 15 | 32 | 52 | 70 | 81 |

(a) Plot the points and draw a line of best fit.
Estimate its gradient and $y$-intercept to one significant figure.
Hence find an approximate equation for your line of best fit.
(b) Use your equation to estimate how high the ball would bounce if dropped
from a height of
(i) 65 cm   (ii) 2 m
(c) Which of your estimates will be more reliable? Why?

# Mixed questions 3

1 Calculate the sides and angles marked with letters.

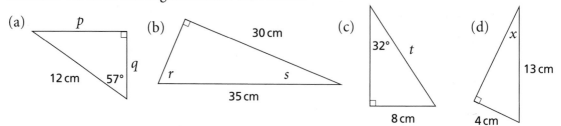

(a) $p$, 12 cm, 57°, $q$  (b) 30 cm, $r$, 35 cm, $s$  (c) 32°, $t$, 8 cm  (d) $x$, 13 cm, 4 cm

2 Find the equation of
  (a) the line parallel to $y = 5x - 3$ going through $(0, 2)$
  (b) the line parallel to $x + 2y = 5$ going through $(0, ^-4)$
  (c) the line perpendicular to $y = x + 3$ going through $(1, 1)$

3 (a) Write 0.000 001 42 in standard form.
  (b) Work out $(4 \times 10^7) \times (3 \times 10^{-3})$, giving the result in standard form.
  (c) Work out $\dfrac{2 \times 10^{-2}}{4 \times 10^4}$, giving the result in standard form.

4 (a) A car travelling at constant speed takes 5 seconds to travel 100 m.
      Find the average speed of the car in kilometres per hour.
  (b) Another car travels at 90 km/h. How long, in seconds, does it take to travel 100 m?

5 How many litres of water will this skip contain when it is full?

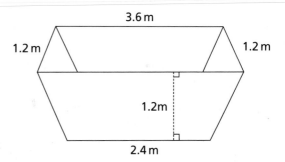

3.6 m, 1.2 m, 1.2 m, 1.2 m, 2.4 m

6 Calculate the angle ABC in this diagram.

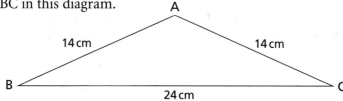

A, 14 cm, 14 cm, B, 24 cm, C

7 Find the value of $n$ in each of these equations.
  (a) $5^3 \times 5^n = 5^6$   (b) $2^n \times 2^5 = 2$   (c) $7^2 \times 7^n = 7^{-2}$   (d) $\dfrac{3^3}{3^n} = 3^5$

**8** ABCD is a kite.

Diagonals AC and BD cross at E.

AB and AD are each of length 5 cm.

BC and CD are each of length 7 cm.

Angle BAD = 128°.

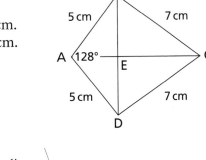

Calculate

(a) BD

(b) angle BCD

**9** ABCD is a rectangle.

Find

(a) the gradient of DC

(b) the equation of AB

(c) the equation of BC

(d) the equation of BD

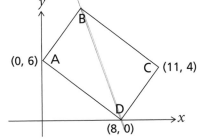

**10** Karen and Asaan both start with the same number.

Karen halves the number and subtracts it from 14.

Asaan adds 7 to the number, then divides the result by 3.

They end up with the same final number.

Find their starting number.

**11** Work out each of these, giving your answer in standard form.

(a) $4 \times 10^5 + 2 \times 10^3$ 　　(b) $4 \times 10^5 - 2 \times 10^3$ 　　(c) $\dfrac{1}{4 \times 10^5}$

**12** (a) An open box consisting of four sides and a base
is made of mahogany with a thickness of 12 mm.

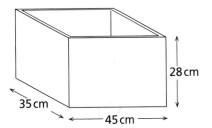

　　(i) Find the volume of the mahogany used by
finding the difference between the total
volume of the box and the internal volume.

　　(ii) The density of mahogany is 0.85 g/cm³.
What is the mass of the box?

　(b) A box with the same dimensions is made of a different wood.
This box has a mass of 5.06 kg. What is the density of this wood?

**\*13** Sam is doing a cycling time trial.

He wants to cover the 20 km distance at an average speed of 40 km/h.

The first 5 km is uphill and he only averages 15 km/h.

What would his average speed need to be for the remainder of the distance
if he is to reach his target?

# 14 *Loci and constructions*

## Section A

1 Mark a point P on paper.
Draw a line *l* through point P.

Draw accurately the locus of points that are 4 cm from point P.
Label it (a).

Draw accurately the locus of points that are 3 cm from line *l*.
Label it (b).

Shade the locus of points that are 4 cm or less from P and 3 cm or more from *l*.

2 Draw rectangle ABCD.

Show how to find, using only straight-edge
and compasses, the point on diagonal BD
that is equidistant from lines AB and AD.

3 (a) Draw parallelogram PQRS.

Show how to find, using only straight-edge
and compasses, the point on line PQ
that is equidistant from points R and S.

(b) Draw parallelogram PQRS again.

Show how to find, using only straight-edge
and compasses, the point on line PQ
that is equidistant from points Q and S.

(c) Draw parallelogram PQRS again.

Show how to find, using only straight-edge
and compasses, the point on line RS
that is equidistant from lines PQ and PS.

4 Draw a circle and mark three points A, B, C on it.

Construct the locus of all the points inside the
circle that are nearer to A than to either B or C.

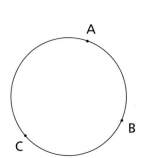

## Section B

**1** A yard is in the shape of a rectangle ABCD.
AB = 10 m and BC = 6 m.

A small animal is tethered to point A by
a rope 8 m long.

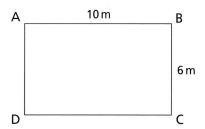

(a) Draw a plan of the yard to scale and shade
the part that the animal can reach.

(b) Explain how to find the point where the
animal is closest to C.

**2** Draw this rectangle accurately.

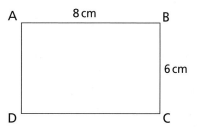

(a) Shade the locus of points that are
closer to line AB than to line BC and
are closer to point C than to point A.

(b) Mark a point Q, which is equidistant from
lines AB and AD, and is 4 cm from line CD.

**3** This is a plan of a room.

An infra-red detector is to be fitted high up on
one of the walls.
It must be placed so that it can 'see' the whole room.

Copy the plan.
Mark with a dotted line those parts of the walls
where the detector could be fitted.

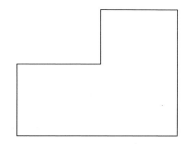

**4** The diagram shows the plan of a rectangular garden.

There is a treasure buried in the garden.
The following facts are known about its position.

It is more than 12 m from D.

It is nearer to A than to C.

It is nearer to CD than to BC.

Draw the plan to scale and shade the part
where the treasure could be buried.

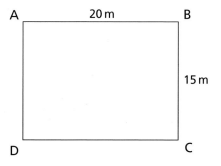

**5** A quadrilateral has a point inside it that is equidistant from all four sides.

Say whether the quadrilateral could be each of these,
illustrating each answer with a sketch.

(a) A square

(b) A rectangle that is not a square

(c) A rhombus

(d) A parallelogram that is not a rhombus

(e) A kite that is not a rhombus

(f) A trapezium that is not a rhombus

# 15 Cumulative frequency

## Section C

1 A mouse breeder likes to weigh all his mice every week as a check on their health. Here is the cumulative frequency graph of his results for one week.

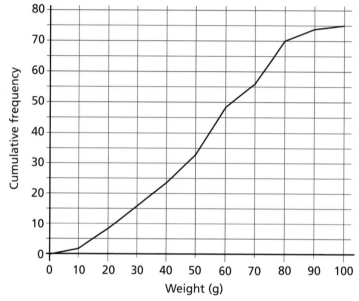

(a) Use the graph to estimate how many mice weigh up to

   (i) 25 g          (ii) 45 g          (iii) 65 g          (iv) 85 g

(b) Estimate the percentage of mice that weigh

   (i) up to 25 g    (ii) up to 45 g    (iii) over 65 g    (iv) over 45 g

   (v) between 50 g and 90 g

(c) Estimate the weight that 80% of the mice are below.

2 This table gives information about the midday temperatures at a holiday resort each day for a year.

| Temperature ($T$°C) | Frequency |
|---|---|
| $-10 < T \le 0$ | 3 |
| $0 < T \le 10$ | 83 |
| $10 < T \le 20$ | 196 |
| $20 < T \le 30$ | 80 |
| $30 < T \le 40$ | 3 |

(a) Make a table of cumulative frequencies.

(b) Draw a cumulative frequency graph.

(c) Estimate the number of days for which the temperature was between 15°C and 25°C.

(d) Estimate what percentage of the days had temperatures over 23°C.

## Section D

1  This graph shows the cumulative frequency curve for the marks of 160 students.

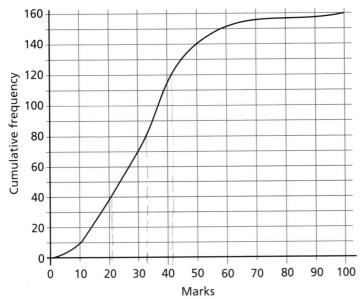

Marks

From the graph estimate

(a) the median mark

(b) the lower quartile

(c) the upper quartile

(d) the interquartile range

(e) the pass mark if three-quarters of the students passed

(f) the number of students achieving more than 30 marks

2  Here are the heights of some pupils in a school.

| Height ($h$ cm) | Frequency |
|---|---|
| $140 < h \leq 145$ | 3 |
| $145 < h \leq 150$ | 5 |
| $150 < h \leq 155$ | 10 |
| $155 < h \leq 160$ | 12 |
| $160 < h \leq 165$ | 15 |
| $165 < h \leq 170$ | 6 |
| $170 < h \leq 175$ | 3 |
| $175 < h \leq 180$ | 2 |

(a) Draw up a cumulative frequency table.

(b) Draw the cumulative frequency graph.

(c) Use the graph to estimate

   (i)  the median

   (ii) the quartiles

   (iii) the interquartile range

3  Calculate an estimate of the mean height of the pupils in question 2.

*4  The speeds in m.p.h. of 200 cars travelling along a particular road were measured. The results are shown in this table.

| Speed ($s$ m.p.h.) | $s \leq 20$ | $s \leq 25$ | $s \leq 30$ | $s \leq 35$ | $s \leq 40$ | $s \leq 45$ | $s \leq 50$ | $s \leq 55$ | $s \leq 60$ |
|---|---|---|---|---|---|---|---|---|---|
| Cumulative frequency | 1 | 7 | 16 | 30 | 64 | 110 | 167 | 188 | 200 |

Calculate an estimate for the mean speed of the cars, showing your method.

## Section E

1 Draw a box-and-whisker plot to show this information about the weights of 60 family bags of crisps.

*A quarter of the bags weighed 142 g or less, the lightest being 123 g.*
*A quarter of the bags weighed 151 g or more, the heaviest being 163 g.*
*The median weight was 148 g.*

2 These box-and-whisker plots show the number of hours per week that men and women worked in 1999.
Write a couple of sentences comparing the hours worked by men and women.

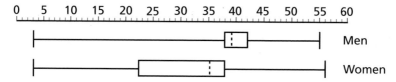

3 These graphs show the results of two tests taken by the same group.

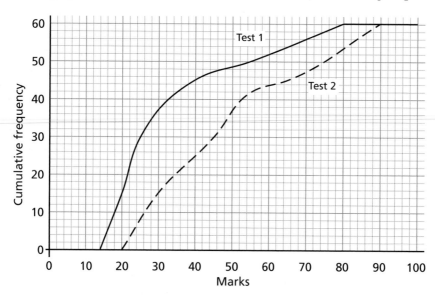

(a) Find the median and quartiles for each test.
(b) Draw two box-and-whisker plots, one for each test.
(c) Write down the interquartile range for each test.
(d) Write a couple of sentences comparing the two sets of results.
(e) If the pass mark was 55%, how many passed each test?

# 16 Combining transformations

## Section A

1 Describe the translation needed to transform the shaded shape on to each of the lettered shapes.

2 Copy the grid and the shaded shape.
   Show where the shaded shape would be after a translation using these vectors.

   (a) $\begin{bmatrix} 1 \\ 2 \end{bmatrix}$ Label it P.  (b) $\begin{bmatrix} -4 \\ 1 \end{bmatrix}$ Label it Q.

   (c) $\begin{bmatrix} -3 \\ -3 \end{bmatrix}$ Label it R.  (d) $\begin{bmatrix} 0 \\ -2 \end{bmatrix}$ Label it S.

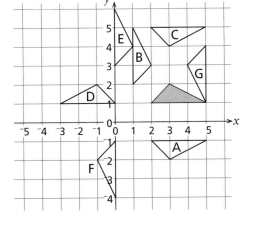

3 After a transformation point $(a, b)$ moves to $(a - 4, b + 2)$.
   What is the vector of this translation?

4 Where would point $(2, -3)$ end up after a translation $\begin{bmatrix} -1 \\ 5 \end{bmatrix}$?

5 Describe the reflection needed to transform the shaded triangle into each of the lettered shapes.

6 Copy the grid and the shaded triangle.
   Show where the shaded triangle would be after a reflection in each of the following lines.

   (a) $y = -1$.     Label it H.
   (b) $x = 0$.     Label it I.
   (c) $y = -x$.     Label it J.
   (d) $y = 2 - x$.  Label it K.
   (e) $y = x - 1$.  Label it L.

7 (a) Copy this shape and reflect it in the $x$-axis.
   (b) Copy it again and reflect it in the $y$-axis.
   (c) Copy it again and reflect it in the line $y = x$.

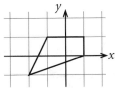

8 Where do these points move to after reflection in the given lines?

   (a) $(2, 4)$, line $y = x$      (b) $(-6, 0)$, line $y = x$
   (c) $(3, 5)$, line $x = 0$      (d) $(1, -4)$, line $y = 0$

9 By testing with some coordinates, give the image of point $(a, b)$ after reflection in the following lines.

   (a) $y = 2$      (b) $y = -x$      (c) $y = x + 1$      (d) $y = 2 - x$

**10** Describe fully the rotations needed to transform the shaded shape on to each of the lettered shapes.

**11** Copy the grid and shaded shape. Show the effect of these rotations on the shaded shape.

G   180° about (0, 1)
H   ⁻90° about (1, 4)
I   ⁺90 about (3, 3)
J   ⁻90° about (0, ⁻1)
K   180° about (⁻1½, 3)
L   ⁻90° about (⁻4, 2)

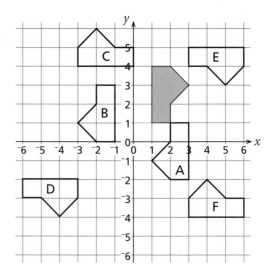

**12** Look at the shapes drawn on this grid. Describe carefully the transformation that would take

(a) A to B

(b) C to D

(c) A to C

(d) A to D

(e) A to F

(f) E to A

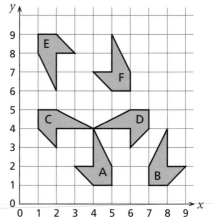

**13** Copy the grid and the shaded shape. Show the results of these transformations of the shaded shape.

(a) Reflection in the line $y = 2$. Label it A.

(b) Translation by the vector $\begin{bmatrix} 3 \\ 1 \end{bmatrix}$. Label it B.

(c) Rotation by 180° about (3, 2). Label it C.

(d) Translation by the vector $\begin{bmatrix} -3 \\ 0 \end{bmatrix}$. Label it D.

(e) Reflection in the line $y = ⁻x$. Label it E.

(f) Rotation 90° anticlockwise about the origin. Label it F.

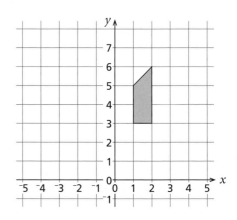

**14** Look at your diagram for question 13. Describe the transformation that would take

(a) shape A to C          (b) shape E to F          (c) shape D to B

(d) shape D to F          (e) shape A to E

**15** Write down the coordinates of the point to which $(2, 6)$ will be transformed after a rotation about $(0, 0)$ of (a) $180°$ (b) $^+90°$ (c) $^-90°$

**16** What will be the image of point $(a, b)$ after each of the rotations in question 15?

# Section B

**1** Use a ruler to draw a capital letter A about the same size as this one, approximately in the centre of a piece of plain paper.
Mark a point O in the centre of the bottom of the A.

Using O as the centre of enlargement, enlarge your letter A using scale factor (a) 2 (b) $\frac{1}{2}$ (c) $^-1$

**2** On another sheet of plain paper, draw a capital N in the centre.
Mark point O slightly to the left, again on the bottom line of the N.

Using O as the centre of enlargement, enlarge your letter N using scale factor (a) 2 (b) $-\frac{1}{2}$ (c) $^-2$

**3** On squared paper draw a grid with both axes from $^-8$ to 8.
Draw the triangle with vertices A $(2, 2)$, B $(3, 4)$, C $(^-1, 4)$.

Draw the following enlargements of this triangle, all with centre $(0, 0)$.

(a) Scale factor 2. Label it A′B′C′.  (b) Scale factor $\frac{1}{2}$. Label it A″B″C″.

(c) Scale factor $^-1$. Label it A‴B‴C‴.

(d) What other transformation would take ABC on to A‴B‴C‴?

**4** Draw another grid from $^-8$ to 8 on both axes.
Draw the shape with vertices $(^-1, ^-1)$, $(3, ^-1)$, $(3, 2)$, $(1, 3)$, $(^-1, 2)$.
Enlarge this shape with the following scale factors, all with centre $(0, 0)$.
(Your shapes may overlap each other.)

(a) 2  (b) $\frac{1}{2}$  (c) $^-1$

**5** The shaded triangle on this grid has been enlarged to make the other triangles.
For each labelled triangle, state the scale factor of the enlargement, and its centre.

**6** Draw a grid from $^-8$ to 8 for both axes and draw the shape with vertices $(4, 2)$, $(6, 3)$, $(6, 4)$, $(2, 3)$.

Shade this shape and then enlarge it with

(a) scale factor $^-1$, centre $(0, 1)$

(b) scale factor 2, centre $(4, 6)$

(c) scale factor $\frac{1}{2}$, centre $(^-4, 7)$

(d) scale factor $^-2$, centre $(2, 1)$

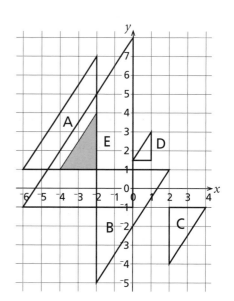

## Section C

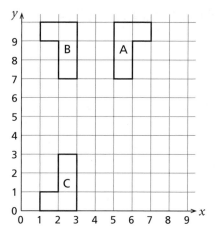

1 (a) Describe the transformation that takes shape A to shape B.

(b) Describe the transformation that takes shape B to shape C.

(c) Describe the **single** transformation that takes shape A to shape C.

2 (a) On a ⁻6 to 6 grid draw the shape with vertices A (1, 2), B (3, 3), C (⁻1, 5), D (⁻1, 2).

(b) Reflect the shape in the line x = 2 and label it A′B′C′D′.

(c) Reflect A′B′C′D′ in the line y = 1 and label it A″B″C″D″.

(d) What **single** transformation maps ABCD on to A″B″C″D″?

3 What single transformation is equivalent to a reflection in the line y = ⁻3 followed by a reflection in the line x = 5?

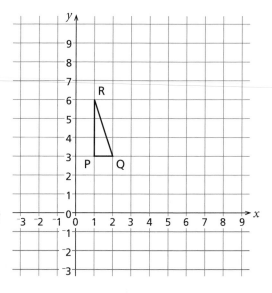

4 (a) Copy the grid and triangle PQR.

(b) Rotate the triangle 90° clockwise about the origin. Label this triangle P′Q′R′.

(c) Reflect triangle P′Q′R′ in the x-axis. Label it P″Q″R″.

(d) Describe the single transformation that would take triangle PQR directly to triangle P″Q″R″.

(e) What would the effect be if the reflection in the x-axis had been done before the rotation of 90° clockwise about the origin? Illustrate your answer.

5 Draw a grid from ⁻9 to 9 for both axes.
Draw the shape with vertices (⁻1, 1), (⁻3, 1), (⁻3, 2), (⁻2, 3).
Label this shape A.

(a) Enlarge shape A by scale factor ⁻2, centre (1, 1). Label this shape B.

(b) Enlarge shape B by scale factor $\frac{1}{2}$, centre (⁻3, ⁻7). Label this shape C.

(c) Describe the single transformation that would take shape A to shape C.

# 17 Probability

## Section B

1 Carla writes numbers on the faces of a regular octahedron.
She rolls the octahedron many times
and makes this record of how it lands.

| Number uppermost | 1 | 2 | 3 | 4 |
|---|---|---|---|---|
| Frequency | | 85 | 124 | 35 | 76 |

What numbers do you think she wrote on the eight faces of the octahedron?

2 Mark catches the train to work every day.
He keeps a record of the train's punctuality.

| Punctuality | early | on time | less than 10 minutes late | between 10 and 30 minutes late | 30 minutes or more late |
|---|---|---|---|---|---|
| Frequency | 8 | 91 | 110 | 28 | 13 |

(a) What is the probability that the train is early or on time?

(b) Mark gets compensation if the train is 30 minutes or more late.
What is the probability that he gets compensation?

## Section C

1 One of these cards is picked at random.

14　15　16　17　18　19　20　21　22　23

Event J is 'The number picked is less than 20'.
Event K is 'The number picked is prime'.
Event L is 'The number picked is a multiple of 7'.
Event M is 'The number picked is a multiple of 4'.

(a) Are these pairs of events mutually exclusive?

(i) J, K　　(ii) J, L　　(iii) K, L　　(iv) K, M　　(v) L, M

(b) What is the probability that the number picked is

(i) either less than 20 or prime　　(ii) either a multiple of 7 or a multiple of 4

(iii) either prime or a multiple of 4　　(iv) either even or a multiple of 7

2 A fairground game involves picking a card at random from a pack of playing cards.
A winning card is either an ace or a picture card (king, queen, jack).

Marie said　'The probability of picking an ace is $\frac{4}{52}$.
The probability of picking a picture card is $\frac{12}{52}$,
so the probability of picking a winning card is $\frac{16}{52}$.'

Is she right? Explain your answer.

## Sections D and E

1  Darren spins a coin twice.
   What is the probability that Darren gets a head

   (a) on the first spin

   (b) on the second spin

   (c) on both the first and the second spin

2  In a game a player must roll an ordinary dice and spin the spinner.

   (a) What is the probability that

       (i)   the spinner shows red

       (ii)  the dice shows 4

       (iii) the spinner shows red and the dice shows 4

       (iv)  the spinner shows blue and the dice shows 3

   (b) The player has another go if the dice shows an even number
       and the spinner shows green.
       What is the probability of having another go?

3  The probability of winning on a slot machine is $\frac{1}{15}$.
   Lisa has two goes on the slot machine.

   (a) Copy and complete the tree diagram
       for two goes on the slot machine,
       writing the probabilities on the branches.

   (b) Find the probability that Lisa wins on both goes.

   (c) Find the probability that Lisa wins on only one of her goes.

   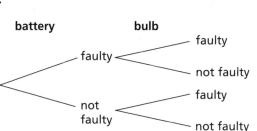

4  Kieran fits the battery and bulb into torches.
   The probability that the battery is faulty is 0.1.
   The probability that the bulb is faulty is 0.3.

   (a) Copy and complete the
       tree diagram for the torch.

   (b) The torch is faulty if either the
       battery or the bulb is faulty.
       What is the probability
       that the torch is faulty?

## Section F

1 A box contains 4 black counters and 3 white counters.
Two counters are taken out at random without replacement.
Find the probability that
   (a) both counters are black
   (b) both counters are the same colour
   (c) the counters are different colours

2 People who want a widgeter's licence have to take two tests: theory and practical.
The probability of passing the theory test is $\frac{2}{5}$.

If a person passes the theory test, the probability of passing the practical test is $\frac{3}{5}$.
If a person fails the theory test, the probability of passing the practical test is $\frac{1}{10}$.
   (a) What is the probability of passing both tests?
   (b) What is the probability of passing just one of the tests, but not both?

3 Meteorologists in Xanadu have noticed a pattern in the weather.
Days are either dry or wet.

If one day is dry, the probability that the next day is dry is $\frac{1}{3}$.

If one day is wet, the probability that the next day is wet is $\frac{3}{4}$.

Given that today is dry, what is the probability
that the day after tomorrow is wet?

## Section G

1 The table shows the results when a group
of adults and children were asked whether
they own a mobile phone.

|  | Owns a mobile phone | Does not own a mobile phone |
|---|---|---|
| Child | 13 | 6 |
| Adult | 11 | 15 |

Find the probability that
   (a) a person chosen at random from this group owns a mobile phone
   (b) a child chosen at random from this group does not own a mobile phone
   (c) a person chosen at random who does not own a mobile phone is an adult
   (d) a child and an adult, both chosen at random, both own a mobile phone

2 The probability of bus A being late is 0.2.
Independently the probability of bus B being late is 0.3.
What is the probability of at least one of the buses being late?

65

# 18 *Simultaneous equations*

## Sections B and C

1 Solve these pairs of equations.

  (a) $x + 3y = 15$
     $x + 6y = 21$

  (b) $2x - y = 14$
     $x + y = 10$

  (c) $y = x + 4$
     $y + 3x = 12$

2 Find two numbers whose sum is 56 and whose difference is 32.

3 Solve these pairs of equations.

  (a) $x + 3y = 11$
     $2x + y = 2$

  (b) $3x - y = 11$
     $x - 2y = 7$

  (c) $3x + 5y = {}^-3$
     $5x - 2y = 26$

4 Two apples and three bananas cost 85p.
  Five apples and a banana cost £1.15.

  Form two equations and solve them to find the cost of an apple and the cost of a banana.

5 Hayley was sent to the shops with £2 to buy 6 oranges and 4 apples.
  Unfortunately she bought 4 oranges and 6 apples and received 18p change.
  If she had bought the correct number of oranges and apples she would
  have received 12p change.

  Form two equations and solve them to find the cost of   (a) an orange   (b) an apple

6 Amy bought 6 kg of potatoes for £5.08.
  Some of the potatoes were red and some white.
  The red potatoes cost 90p per kg and the white potatoes cost 80p per kg.

  How many kilograms of each kind of potatoes did she buy?

7 Half the sum of two numbers is 51. The difference between them is 36.
  Find the two numbers.

8 Solve these pairs of equations.

  (a) $4x + y = 3$
     $2x - 3y = 12$

  (b) $x + 2y = 11$
     $2x + 3y = 14$

  (c) $3x - 2y = 4$
     $x - 3y = 13$

  (d) $2x - 3y = 11$
     $3x + 4y = 8$

  (e) $5x - 3y = 15$
     $3x - 5y = 17$

  (f) $7x + 3y = 7$
     $x - 5y = 20$

9 I am thinking of two numbers.
  If I add 15 to the first number I get twice the second number.
  If I add 21 to the second number I get twice the first number.

  What are my two numbers?

**10** The picture shows a piece of trellis made from 7 m of timber.
The perimeter of the trellis is 3.2 m.

What are the dimensions of the trellis?

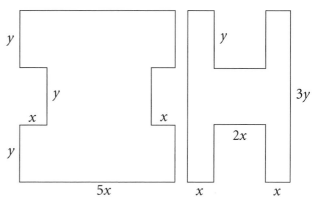

**11** A piece of wire of length 184 cm can be bent to form either of these shapes.

Find lengths $x$ and $y$.

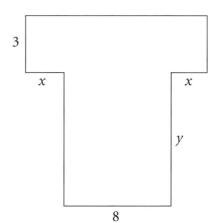

**12** The area of this T-shaped piece of card is 116 cm² and the perimeter is 51 cm.

Find lengths $x$ and $y$.

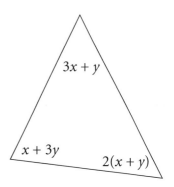

**13** Find $x$ and $y$ for these triangles.

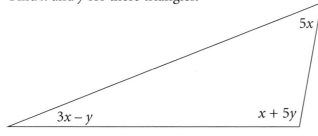

## Section D

**1** (a)  Rearrange the equation $2x + y = 20$ in the form $y = .....$

    (b)  By substituting your answer for (a) into the equation $3x + 2y = 33$, solve the pair of simultaneous equations $2x + y = 20$, $3x + 2y = 33$.

**2** Solve these pairs of simultaneous equations by the substitution method.

    (a)  $3x + y = 3$
         $4x + 5y = 26$

    (b)  $3x + 2y = 11$
         $y - 2x - 9 = 0$

    (c)  $x - y = 5$
         $5x + 3y = 13$

## Section E

Use these graphs to answer the questions below.

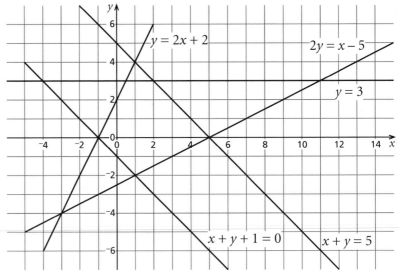

**1** (a)  Which pair of these equations does not have a solution?

    (b)  Why not?

**2** (a)  How many solutions are possible for this pair of simultaneous equations?

$$y = 5 - x$$
$$x + y = 5$$

    (b)  Give a reason for your answer.

**3** Use the graphs to solve the following pairs of simultaneous equations.

    (a)  $y = 2x + 2$
         $x + y = 5$

    (b)  $2y = x - 5$
         $y = 3$

    (c)  $x + y = 5$
         $y - 3 = 0$

    (d)  $y - 2x = 2$
         $x + y + 1 = 0$

    (e)  $y = 2x + 2$
         $y = \frac{x}{2} - \frac{5}{2}$

    (f)  $x + y = {}^-1$
         $2y - x + 5 = 0$

    (g)  $y = 3$
         $x + y = {}^-1$

    (h)  $x + y - 5 = 0$
         $2y + 5 = x$

## Section F

1  A country show lasted three days.
   The cost of admission on the first two days was £5 and it was reduced
   to £3 for the final day.
   8400 people attended the show.
   £37 000 was paid for admission over the three days.

   How many people attended on the final day?

2  The cost of entry to a football match was £15 and £12.
   1000 more people paid the higher price than the lower price.
   £244 500 was paid for tickets.

   How many people attended the match?

   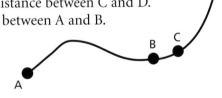

   **NEWCHESTER UNITED**
   North & South Stands: £15
   East & West Stands: £12

3  A fraction has a value of $\frac{1}{2}$ when 1 is added to the numerator.
   The fraction's value is $\frac{1}{3}$ when 1 is added to the denominator.

   Find the fraction.

4  If you add 1 to the numerator of a fraction, it has a value of $\frac{1}{4}$.
   It also has a value of $\frac{1}{4}$ if you subtract 4 from the denominator.

   Find the fraction.
   Is there more than one possible solution?

5  Four towns A, B, C and D are connected by a railway line.
   The distance between A and C is three times the distance between C and D.
   The distance between B and D is half the distance between A and B.
   B and C are 5 km apart.

   Find the distance from A to B and from C to D.

*6  A motorist driving to London averages 60 km per hour in the country
    and 20 km per hour in the towns.
    The journey takes her 4 hours.
    When she drives home she averages 50 km per hour in the country
    and 15 km per hour in the towns.
    The journey takes her 5 hours and 4 minutes.

    How long was her journey to London?

*7  A man walks from home 15 km up and down some hills and then back
    home along the same route.
    When he walks uphill he walks at an average speed of 3 km per hour.
    When he walks downhill he walks at an average speed of 5 km per hour.
    The return journey takes 8 minutes longer than the outward journey.

    On his outward journey, how many kilometres are uphill?

# Mixed questions 4

**1** This cumulative frequency table gives information about the age distribution of the population of a country.

| Age (a years) | a ≤ 10 | a ≤ 20 | a ≤ 40 | a ≤ 60 | a ≤ 80 | a ≤ 100 |
|---|---|---|---|---|---|---|
| Cumulative frequency (in millions) | 2 | 5 | 10 | 23 | 37 | 44 |

(a) What is the total population of the country?

(b) How many people are in the following age intervals?

   (i) $10 < a \leq 20$      (ii) $20 < a \leq 40$      (iii) $40 < a \leq 100$

(c) Calculate an estimate of the mean age of the population.

**2** (a) Copy this diagram.
Rotate the flag F through 180° about A.
Draw the image and label it F′.

(b) Rotate F′ through 180° about B.
Draw the image and label it F″.

(c) Describe fully the single transformation that maps F on to F″.

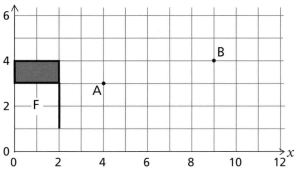

**3** Two groups of people visited a theme park.
The first group consisted of 3 adults and 5 children and paid £26.
The second group consisted of 2 adults and 6 children and paid £24.

By setting up and solving a pair of simultaneous equations, calculate the cost of an adult ticket and the cost of a child ticket.

**4** (a) A box contains 1 red counter, 2 blue counters and 3 green counters.
Sally takes a counter at random from the box and notes its colour.
She then puts it back in the box, shakes the box and again takes a counter at random.
Find the probability that both counters she takes are the same colour.

(b) As before, the box contains 1 red, 2 blue and 3 green counters.
Sally takes a counter at random from the box but does not put it back.
Then she takes a second counter at random from those that are left.
Find the probability that both counters she takes are the same colour.

**5** ABCD is a trapezium. AB is parallel to DC, but AD is not parallel to BC.

Show how to construct a point that is equidistant from AB and DC, and also equidistant from AD and BC.

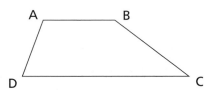

# 19 *Solving inequalities*

## Section A

1 Copy and complete the following by replacing □ with the correct symbol, <, > or = .

   (a) $3 \, \square \, \pi$        (b) $7 \, \square \, \sqrt{7}$        (c) $4^2 \, \square \, 9$        (d) $3 \, \square \, \sqrt{9}$

2 Match the inequalities with the diagrams.

   (a) $n > 3$        (b) $n \leq 3$        (c) $3 > n$        (d) $3 \leq n$

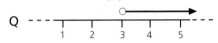

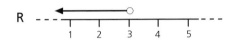

3 Draw number lines to show these inequalities.

   (a) $0 < n \leq 2$        (b) $^-5 \leq n < {}^-2$        (c) $4 \leq n \leq 6$        (d) $6 < n < 12$

4 List all the integers satisfied by these inequalities.

   (a)    [number line from 1 to 9, open circle at 2, closed circle at 7]      (b) $0 < n < 6$

   (c)    [number line from −1 to 7, open circle at 0, closed circle at 5]      (d) $10 \geq n \geq 6$

   (e) $^-1.2 < n < 0$                   (f) $1.8 \leq n \leq 2.6$

5 Write down the five integers, $n$, such that $n^2 \leq 4$.

6 List all the square numbers, $s$, such that $0 < s < 20$.

7 List all the factors, $f$, of 24 such that $1 < f < 8$.

8 (a) If $a$ stands for the size of an angle in degrees, write inequalities for each of these statements.

     (i) The angle is less than 90°.

     (ii) The angle is between 90° and 180°.

     (iii) The angle is greater than 180°.

   (b) What is the special name given to the angles in each case?

9 If $l$ stands for the weight of a letter in grams, write inequalities for each of these statements.

   (a) The letter weighs 60 g or less.

   (b) The letter weighs more than 60 g up to and including 100 g.

   (c) The letter weighs over 100 g.

## Section C

**1** Match the inequalities with number-line solutions.

(a) $x + 3 \geq 7$  (b) $x - 1 < 7$  (c) $\frac{x}{2} \leq 4$  (d) $0 > x - 9$

P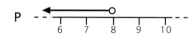

Q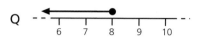

R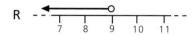

S

**2** Solve the following inequalities and show each solution on a number line.

(a) $x + 2 < 1$  (b) $5x \leq 10$  (c) $6 < x - 3$

**3** Solve the following inequalities.

(a) $3a - 7 < 8$  (b) $6 + 2b \geq 4$  (c) $7 > 2c - 5$

(d) $d - 8 \leq 6$  (e) $9 \leq 12 + 3e$  (f) $\frac{f}{2} + 5 > 7$

(g) $4 + \frac{g}{4} \leq 6$  (h) $3h + 9 > 0$  (i) $0 \leq 1 + \frac{i}{2}$

**4** Solve each of these.

(a) $3r > r + 7$  (b) $5s \leq s - 8$  (c) $4m + 6 \leq 8m$

(d) $2n - 5 > n$  (e) $4p + 2 \geq 3p$  (f) $2z \leq \frac{z}{2} + 3$

(g) $9l < 4 + l$  (h) $16 + 3q > q$  (i) $\frac{k}{4} + 3 < k$

**5** Solve these by first adding the expression in square brackets to both sides.

(a) $3 - j > 2$  [j]  (b) $8 - 2v \leq 4$  [2v]

(c) $9 < 8 - 4t$  [4t]  (d) $6 - 2w \geq 3 - 3w$  [3w]

**6** Solve these inequalities.

(a) $3s + 6 > 4s + 1$  (b) $4k - 2 < 5k + 1$  (c) $5f - 8 \geq 3f - 2$

(d) $13 + 2g < 3 + 7g$  (e) $23 - 3h \leq 3 + 7h$  (f) $14 - p > 4 - 2p$

(g) $d + 12 \geq 4 - 3d$  (h) $\frac{w}{3} \geq 14 - 2w$  (i) $7 - \frac{n}{2} \geq 27 - 3n$

**7** Multiply out the brackets and then solve the inequalities.

(a) $2(x + 2) < 3x + 1$  (b) $2(x + 4) > 3(x + 1)$  (c) $3(2x - 1) \geq 5x$

(d) $3(10 - x) \leq 2(2x + 1)$  (e) $5(3 + x) < 2(4 - x)$  (f) $3(3 + 4x) > 2(x + 7)$

**8** First multiply both sides of these inequalities by the number in square brackets, and then solve the inequalities.

(a) $\frac{n+2}{4} < n - 4$  [4]  (b) $\frac{n-3}{2} \geq 6 - n$  [2]  (c) $n - 1 > \frac{n+1}{3}$  [3]

(d) $\frac{2n+1}{2} > \frac{4n-1}{3}$  [6]  (e) $\frac{5-n}{3} > \frac{6-n}{2}$  [6]  (f) $\frac{4-n}{2} \leq \frac{2-5n}{4}$  [4]

## Section D

1 Solve these inequalities and show your solutions on a number line.

(a) $0 \leq 3x < 15$      (b) $^-3 < 2x + 1 < 3$      (c) $2 < \frac{x}{2} < 4$

2 List all the integers, $n$, such that

(a) $2 < 3n - 4 \leq 11$      (b) $1 \leq \frac{n}{2} + 2 < 4$      (c) $^-11 < 4n + 5 \leq 5$

3 Find the smallest integer value of $n$ such that

(a) $3(2n - 5) > n + 3$      (b) $5 - 2n < \frac{1}{3}n$      (c) $3(5 - n) < 20$

4 Which of the two inequalities, A or B, do each of these values of $x$ satisfy?

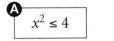   

(a) $x = 2$      (b) $x = ^-1$      (c) $x = 0$

(d) $x = 3$      (e) $x = ^-2.6$      (f) $x = ^-3$

5 Find all the integers such that $x^2 \leq 9$ and $x^2 > 3$.

6 Solve the inequality $x^2 < 36$.
Represent the solution on a number line.

7 Which of these diagrams represents the solution to the inequality $x^2 + 4 \leq 40$?

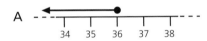   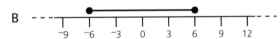

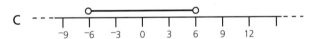

8 Match the inequalities with the number-line solutions.

(a) $x^2 + 8 > 33$      (b) $2x^2 \leq 72$      (c) $3x^2 - 50 < 25$      (d) $7 + 2x^2 \geq 25$

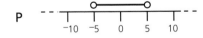   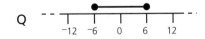

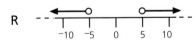   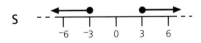

9 Solve the inequality $(x - 2)^2 \leq 25$.

## 20 Brackets and quadratic equations 1

### Section A

**1** Simplify these.

(a) $5h + 3g - 4h - 7g$  (b) $p^2 + 6p - 8p + 12$

(c) $4j \times jk$  (d) $3t \times 5t^2 \times t^3$

**2** Multiply these out and simplify them where possible.

(a) $7x(4x - 3)$  (b) $y(3y^4 + y)$

(c) $4ab(6a - 3b)$  (d) $5p(6 + p) - 4p(2p - 1)$

(e) $3(k - 5) + k(k + 4)$  (f) $7(4 - 2e) - (3 + e)$

**3** Find pairs of expressions from the cloud that multiply
to give the expressions below.

(a) $8p^2q$

(b) $18p - 6p^2q$

(c) $3pq^2 - 9q$

(d) $6p - 2p^2q$

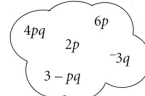

**4** Multiply out and simplify these.

(a) $\frac{1}{3}x \times 9y$  (b) $\frac{1}{2}p \times \frac{1}{4}pq$

(c) $\frac{1}{3}(6x + 3) + \frac{1}{4}(8x - 12)$  (d) $4s\left(\frac{1}{3}t - \frac{1}{5}s\right)$

**5** Find the missing expressions to make these statements correct.

(a) $3y(4y - \Box) = 12y^2 - 9y$  (b) $\Box(3p + q) = 9p^2q + 3pq^2$

**6** Find an expression for the area of each shaded shape.
Give answers in their simplest form.

(a)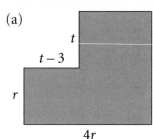

(b)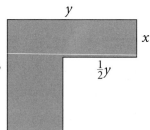

## Section B

1 Factorise these completely.

(a) $6x + 12y$

(b) $st - t^2$

(c) $7y + y^2z$

(d) $30h^2j + 24hj^2$

(e) $3a^2b + 12ab^3$

(f) $4m^2n^3 - 6m^7$

(g) $6pq^2 - 18p^2q^3$

(h) $7ab^3 + 7a^2b^2$

(i) $16x^2y^3 + 4xy^2$

2 (a) Factorise $4n + 8$.

  (b) Explain how the factorisation tells you that $4n + 8$ will be a
      multiple of 4 for any integer $n$.

3 (a) Factorise $n^2 - n$.

  (b) Use the factorisation to explain why $n^2 - n$ will always be even for any integer $n$.

4

| A | E | G | N | O | P | R | S |
|---|---|---|---|---|---|---|---|
| $q - 2$ | $3p$ | $p$ | $p - 3$ | $2q$ | 6 | $p^2 + 3$ | $q^2 - 7$ |

Fully factorise each expression below as the product of two factors.
Use the code above to find the letter for each factor.
Rearrange each set of letters to spell out an item of fruit.

(a) $6p^2 + 18$,  $3pq - 6p$

(b) $pq - 2p$,  $3p^2 - 9p$,  $2p^2q + 6q$

(c) $3pq^2 - 21p$,  $p^3 + 3p$,  $6q - 12$

## Section C

1 Multiply out and simplify these.

(a) $(x + 5)(x + 7)$

(b) $(y - 3)(y + 4)$

(c) $(y + 8)(y - 3)$

(d) $(n - 6)(n - 3)$

2 Solve these equations.

(a) $(n - 3)(n + 4) = n(n - 5)$

(b) $(n - 4)(n - 2) = (n - 5)(n - 3)$

3 For each statement below, decide if it is an identity or an equation.
  Solve each equation. Show each identity is true.

(a) $(n - 3)(n + 8) = n^2 + 13n + 24$

(b) $(n - 8)(n - 4) = n^2 - 12n + 32$

(c) $(n + 5)(n - 2) = n(n + 3) - 10$

**4** Write down the expansions of the following.

    (a) $(x + 4)(x - 4)$                   (b) $(x - 6)(x + 6)$

**5** Expand and simplify these.

    (a) $(x + 3)^2$           (b) $(x - 8)^2$           (c) $(x - y)^2$

**6** Find the length of each side for these right-angled triangles.

    (a) 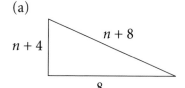           (b)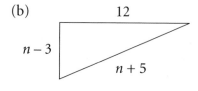

## Section D

**1** Factorise these.

    (a) $n^2 + 7n + 12$       (b) $n^2 + 2n - 15$       (c) $n^2 - 11n + 24$

    (d) $n^2 - 3n - 4$        (e) $n^2 + 5n - 6$

**2** Which of these expressions cannot be factorised using integers only?

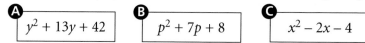

**A** $y^2 + 13y + 42$      **B** $p^2 + 7p + 8$      **C** $x^2 - 2x - 4$      **D** $g^2 - 5g + 4$

**3** Which of the expressions below are perfect squares?

**A** $x^2 + 14x + 4$      **B** $y^2 - 6y + 6$      **C** $x^2 - 12x + 36$      **D** $y^2 - 18y + 81$

**4** (a) Factorise $n^2 + 5n + 6$.

    (b) Hence show that $n^2 + 5n + 6$ must be even for any integer $n$.

**5** The $n$th term of a sequence is $n^2 + 6n + 9$.

    (a) Work out the first five terms of the sequence.

    (b) Show that every term in the infinite sequence must be a square number.

**6** Factorise these.

    (a) $x^2 - 81$          (b) $y^2 - 36$          (c) $n^2 - 121$

**⊠ 7** Evaluate these.

    (a) $29^2 - 1^2$         (b) $29^2$          (c) $49^2$

## Section E

**1** Solve these quadratic equations.

(a) $n^2 + 3n + 2 = 0$  (b) $x^2 - 2x - 48 = 0$

(c) $y^2 + 10y - 24 = 0$  (d) $g^2 + 4g = 0$

(e) $z^2 - 36 = 0$  (f) $p^2 - 24p + 80 = 0$

(g) $r^2 + 4r - 60 = 0$  (h) $t^2 - 20t = 0$

**2** Rearrange and solve these equations.

(a) $h^2 + 10h + 10 = 1$  (b) $x^2 - 3x = 28$

(c) $p^2 - 4p + 3 = 2(p - 1)$  (d) $b(b + 6) = 2(10 - b)$

**3** The width of a rectangle is 5 cm less than the length of the rectangle. The area of the rectangle is 300 cm².

(a) What is the length of the rectangle?

(b) What is the perimeter of the rectangle?

**4** Find the length of each side of this right-angled triangle.

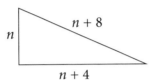

**5** The expression for the $n$th term of a sequence is $n^2 + 3n - 5$.

(a) What is the 5th term of the sequence?

(b) Which term of the sequence is 265?

**6** The dimensions of a rectangle are shown. The rectangle has area 104 cm².

(a) Show that $x$ satisfies the equation $x^2 + 11x - 80 = 0$.

(b) Solve this equation to find the value of $x$.

(c) Write down the perimeter of the rectangle.

**7** The perimeter of a rectangle is 36 cm. The length is $x$ cm.

(a) Write an expression, in terms of $x$, for the width of the rectangle.

(b) Given that the area of the rectangle is 77 cm², form an equation and solve it to find the dimensions of the rectangle.

# 22 *Direct and inverse proportion*

## *Sections B, C and D*

1 This graph shows the mass, $M$ kg, of a type of oil against the volume, $V$ litres.

   (a) What is the equation connecting $M$ and $V$?

   (b) Use the equation to find

      (i) the mass of 8.5 litres of oil

      (ii) the volume of 40.5 kg of oil

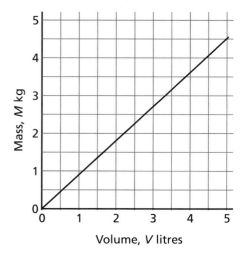

2 $Y$ is directly proportional to $X$.
When $X = 8.0$, $Y = 4.8$.

   (a) Find the equation connecting $Y$ and $X$.

   (b) Calculate  (i) $Y$ when $X = 3.5$    (ii) $X$ when $Y = 10.8$

3 George is a decorator. The amount he charges for painting a ceiling is proportional to the area of the ceiling.

He charges £102.85 for painting a rectangular ceiling 6.8 m by 5.5 m.
How much does he charge for painting a ceiling 4.5 m by 3.6 m?

4 $Q \propto P$ and $Q = 11.2$ when $P = 6.4$.

Calculate  (a) $Q$ when $P = 8.8$    (b) $P$ when $Q = 21.7$

*5 If a gas is kept in a closed container, its pressure is directly proportional to its temperature, when the latter is measured in kelvins (K).

The rule for changing temperatures in °C to K is 'add 273'.
So, for example, 50°C is equivalent to 323 K.

The pressure of the gas in a container at 15°C is 1200 millibars.
What will the pressure be when the container is heated to 250°C?
Give your answer to the nearest 10 millibars.

## Section E

1 The cost, £C, of a metre of cable is proportional to the square of the diameter, $d$ mm.

   (a) Copy this table and fill in the missing values of $d^2$.

   | d | 6 | 10 | 12 | 15 | 20 |
   |---|---|----|----|----|----|
   | d² | 36 | | | | |
   | C | 0.72 | | | | |

   (b) Write the equation connecting $C$ and $d$ in the form $C = kd^2$.

   (c) Using the equation, calculate the missing values of $C$ and enter them in your table.

2 $Q$ is directly proportional to $P^2$.
   When $P = 4$, $Q = 8$.

   (a) Find the equation connecting $Q$ and $P$.

   (b) Find (i) the value of $Q$ when $P = 8$   (ii) the value of $P$ when $Q = 72$

3 A truck is let go and runs down a slope.
   The speed $S$ m/s of the truck is directly proportional to the square root of the distance $D$ m travelled.

   When $D = 3.24$, $S = 1.2$.

   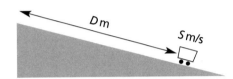

   (a) Find the equation connecting $S$ and $D$.

   (b) Use the equation to calculate   (i) $S$ when $D = 1.44$       (ii) $D$ when $S = 2.0$

4 $Q$ is directly proportional to $P^3$.
   When $P = 5$, $Q = 500$.

   (a) Find the equation connecting $Q$ and $P$.

   (b) Find (i) the value of $Q$ when $P = 4$   (ii) the value of $P$ when $Q = 32$

## Section F

1 When some gas is trapped and compressed, its volume, $V$ litres, is inversely proportional to the pressure, $P$ millibars, applied.

   Here is a table of values of $P$ and $V$.

   | P | 1000 | 1200 | 1600 | 3000 |
   |---|------|------|------|------|
   | V | 4.8 | 4.0 | 3.0 | 1.6 |

   (a) How can you tell from the table that $V$ is inversely proportional to $P$?

   (b) What is the equation connecting $V$ and $P$?

   (c) What is the value of   (i) $V$ when $P = 1500$       (ii) $P$ when $V = 0.96$

2 Given that $Q \propto \frac{1}{P^2}$, and that $Q = 10$ when $P = 5$, find

   (a) the equation connecting $Q$ and $P$       (b) the value of $Q$ when $P = 10$

3 Given that $Y \propto \frac{1}{\sqrt{X}}$, and that $Y = 10$ when $X = 16$, find

   (a) the value of $Y$ when $X = 25$     (b) the value of $X$ when $Y = 20$

# Mixed questions 5

1 If $V$ is inversely proportional to the square of $U$, and $V = 10$ when $U = 2$, find the value of $V$ when $U = 4$.

2 (a) Expand and simplify $(t + 7)(t + 9)$.

(b) By letting $t$ stand for 'ten', use the result in (a) to find the value of $17 \times 19$ without using a calculator.

(c) Expand and simplify $(t + 6)^2$ and use the result to find the value of $16^2$.

(d) Expand and simplify $(t - 4)^2$.
Check that your result gives the correct value when $t = 10$.

(e) Factorise $t^2 + 15t + 36$. Use the result to find a pair of factors of 286.

3 This table shows the age distribution of the members of a club.

| Age group | 15–30 | 30–45 | 45–60 | 60+ |
|---|---|---|---|---|
| Number | 76 | 62 | 31 | 11 |

Reena wants to take a sample of 40 of the members, stratified by age group. How many from each age group should be in the sample?

4 Multiply out the brackets on each side of these equations, then rearrange and solve the equations.

(a) $x(x - 5) = (x + 6)(x - 3)$

(b) $(x - 4)(x - 5) = 2(x - 2)$

5 Solve the following inequalities.

(a) $3 - 2x \geq {}^-5$

(b) $3(x - 2) < 4x + 1$

(c) $\frac{x + 2}{3} \leq 4 - x$

6 (a) A price is increased from £250 to £270. What is the percentage increase?

(b) The price of £270 is increased again, by 15%. What is the new price?

7 Anil's dad is 32 years older than Anil is.
In five years time, Anil's dad will be exactly three times as old as Anil.
How old are Anil and his dad now?

8 Solve the following equations.

(a) $x^2 + 3x + 2 = 0$

(b) $x^2 - 5x - 6 = 0$

(c) $x^2 - 8x + 15 = 0$

9 PQRS is a trapezium with PS parallel to QR.
Angles PQS and QRS are both right angles.
PS = 20 cm and $\sin a = 0.4$.

(a) Calculate QS.

(b) Write down the value of $\cos b$.

(c) Calculate QR.

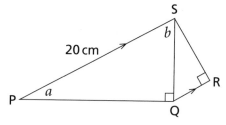

# 23 Graphing inequalities

## Section A

1 Write an inequality for each region that is shaded.

(a)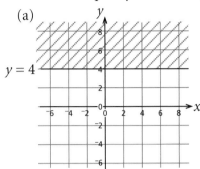

(b)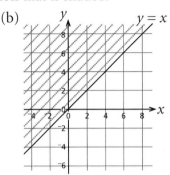

(c)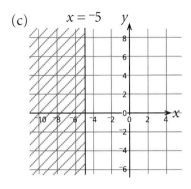

2 Draw a sketch for the region given by each inequality.

(a) $y \geq 0$        (b) $x \leq {}^-2$        (c) $y \geq {}^-4$        (d) $x \geq 2$

3 Write down the inequalities that describe each of the three shaded regions.

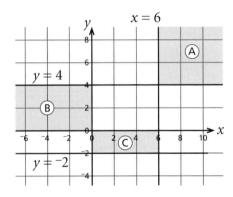

4 On squared paper draw axes with $^-6 \leq x \leq 6$ and $^-6 \leq y \leq 6$.

(a) Shade the region $y \geq 2$.

(b) Shade the region $x \leq 3$.

(c) Shade the region $x \geq {}^-4$.

(d) Label clearly the region which is satisfied by all three inequalities.

## Sections B, C and D

1 For each diagram…

- Write down the equation of the line.
- Write down the inequality which the shaded region (including the line) satisfies.

(a)

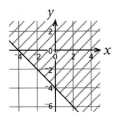

(b)

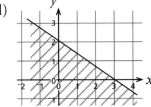

(c)

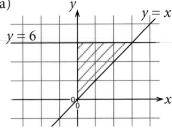

(d)

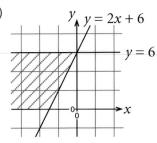

2 On squared paper draw sketches to show clearly the following inequalities.

(a) $3x + 5y \geq 15$        (b) $y \geq 3x - 6$        (c) $3y - 2x \leq 6$

3 Write down the three inequalities which define each shaded region.

(a)

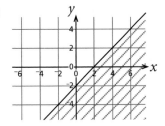

(b)

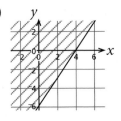

(c)

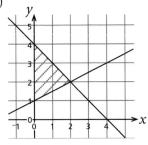

(d)

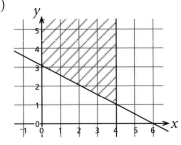

**4** Using squared paper, draw and label axes with $^-2 \le x \le 6$ and $^-2 \le y \le 6$.

Show clearly the single region that is satisfied by all of the following inequalities.

$$x \le 4 \qquad y \le x \qquad y \ge 2$$

**5** Draw and label axes with $^-4 \le x \le 8$ and $^-2 \le y \le 8$.

Draw and shade the region which satisfies both the following inequalities.

$$0 \le y \le 6 \quad \text{and} \quad 2x + 3y \ge 12$$

**6** Draw and label axes with $^-2 \le x \le 5$ and $^-2 \le y \le 4$.

Show clearly the region which satisfies the three inequalities

$$y \le x + 1 \qquad x \le 3 \qquad 3x + 4y \ge 12$$

**7** Write an inequality for each region. The regions do not include any dotted line.

(a)

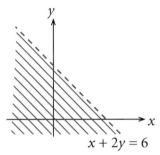

$x + 2y = 6$

(b)

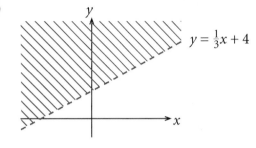

$y = \frac{1}{3}x + 4$

**8** (a) Draw a set of axes with $^-3 \le x \le 7$ and $^-5 \le y \le 6$.

(b) Draw and label the lines

$$y = x + 1 \qquad 4x + 3y = 12 \quad \text{and} \quad x + 2y = {}^-2$$

(c) Shade the region which satisfies all the following inequalities.

$$y < x + 1 \qquad 4x + 3y < 12 \quad \text{and} \quad x + 2y > {}^-2$$

(d) State all the points with integer coordinates which satisfy **all**
the inequalities in part (c).

**9** Write down the three inequalities
satisfied by points in the shaded region
(including boundaries).

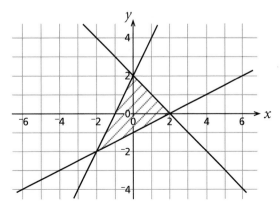

# 25 Length, area and volume

## Section A

**1** Calculate the area and arc length of each of these sectors to one decimal place.

(a)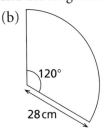
7 cm
36°

(b)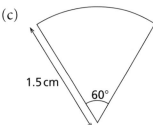
120°
28 cm

(c)
1.5 cm
60°

(d)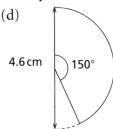
4.6 cm
150°

**2** Calculate the area and arc length of each of these sectors to 1 d.p.

(a)
9 cm
73°

(b)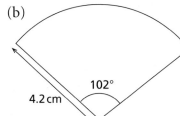
102°
4.2 cm

(c)
3.7 cm
21°

(d)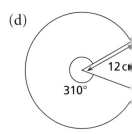
310°
12 cm

**3**

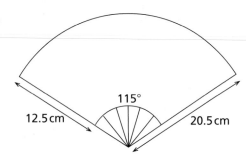
115°
12.5 cm
20.5 cm

(a) Calculate the area of paper used on this open Japanese fan.

(b) Calculate the arc length along the top edge.

(c) How many fans could be made from a single circle of paper of radius 20.5 cm?

## Section B

**1** Calculate the area of each of these isosceles triangles.

(a)
18 cm    18 cm
20 cm

(b)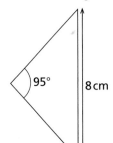
95°
8 cm

(c)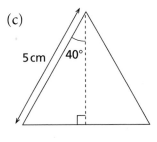
5 cm    40°

**2** Calculate the area of each of the shaded segments.

(a)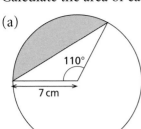

(b)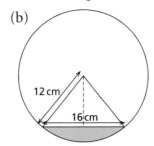

(c)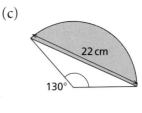

## Section C

**1** Find the volume of each of these cylinders.

(a) Base radius = 2.5 cm, length = 14 cm   (b) Base radius = 7.4 m, length = 0.8 m

(c) Base radius = 10.16 cm, length = 12 m

**2**  This toilet roll has height 11 cm and diameter 12 cm.

The cardboard tube has an internal diameter of 4.5 cm and thickness of 1 mm.

(a) Find the volume of paper on the roll.

(b) There are 280 sheets on the roll which are 12.4 cm by 11 cm. Calculate the thickness of each sheet.

**3** This cake has diameter 20 cm and height 7.5 cm.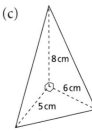

(a) Find the volume of the cake.

The top and the curved surface of the cake will be covered in icing.

(b) Find the area of the surface that will be covered in icing.

(c) The icing is 4 mm thick. Estimate the volume of icing needed, giving your answer to a reasonable degree of accuracy.

**4** What height cylinder of diameter 14 cm would be needed to hold 2 litres of liquid?

## Section D

**1** Calculate the volume of each of these pyramids.

(a)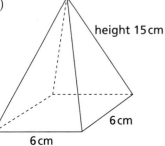
height 15 cm
6 cm
6 cm

(b)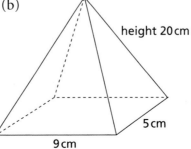
height 20 cm
5 cm
9 cm

(c)
8 cm
6 cm
5 cm

**2** Find the volume of a regular hexagonal-based pyramid of side length 2 cm and height 8 cm.

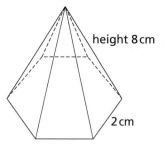

**3** Find the volume of a regular octagonal-based pyramid of side 5 cm and height 25 cm.

**4** Find the volume and curved surface area of each of these cones.

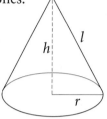

(a) Height = 12 cm, radius = 9 cm, slant height = 15 cm

(b) Height = 27 cm, radius = 12.5 cm

(c) Height = 0.40 m, slant height = 0.50 m

(d) Slant height = 8.3 cm, radius 2.0 cm

(e) Diameter = 9.6 m, height = 21.5 m

**5** A cone of volume 20 000 cm$^3$ has height 30 cm.

(a) Find the radius of the cone to 2 d.p.

(b) Find the curved surface area of the cone to the nearest cm$^2$.

**6** A cone of volume 5000 cm$^3$ has radius 8 cm.
Find the curved surface area of the cone.

## Section E

**1** Calculate the volume and surface area of each of these spheres.

(a) Radius 5 cm      (b) Radius 0.035 m      (c) Radius 12 cm

**2** Calculate the radius of these spheres.

(a) Volume 300 cm$^3$      (b) Surface area 200 cm$^2$      (c) Volume 1000 cm$^3$

**3** Calculate the volume of wood in this rolling pin with hemispherical ends.

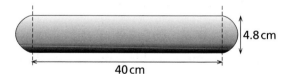

4.8 cm

40 cm

**4** Here is a cross-section of a Malteser.
The diameter of the honeycomb is 1.4 cm.
The thickness of the chocolate covering is 0.1 cm.

Calculate each of these.

(a) The volume of honeycomb

(b) The area of the honeycomb to be covered in chocolate

(c) The volume of the chocolate

# 26 Quadratic graphs

## Section A

**1**

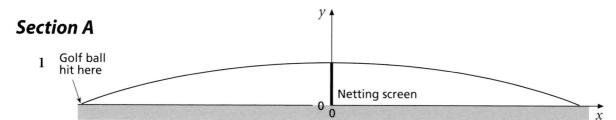

Golf ball hit here

Netting screen

The diagram shows the path of a golf ball.

The equation of the path of the ball is $y = 9 - \dfrac{x^2}{3600}$ ($x$ and $y$ are measured in metres).

(a) The golf ball just clears the netting screen shown.
By putting $x = 0$ in the equation of the path, find how high the screen is.

(b) (i) Find two possible values of $x$ when $y = 0$.

(ii) What do these two values tell you?

(c) How high will the ball be from the ground when it is 110 metres from the point where the golfer hit it?

**2** Two boys are playing with a football in a subway with a ceiling height of 3.5 metres.

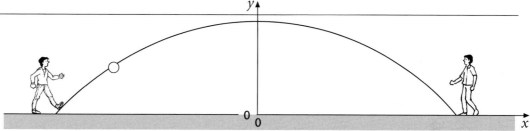

The equation of the path of their football is $y = 3 - \dfrac{x^2}{45}$ ($x$ and $y$ are measured in m).

(a) When they kick the ball would it hit the ceiling?

(b) What is the value of $y$ when $x = 9$?

(c) How far apart are the two boys?

**3** In a game a marble is pushed off the edge of a box.

The equation of the path of the marble is $y = 75 - \dfrac{x^2}{50}$
($x$ and $y$ are measured in cm).

(a) How high is the box?

(b) How far from the bottom of the box does the marble land?

(c) What is the value of $y$ when $x = 25$?

(d) (i) What is the value of $y$ when $x = 70$?

(ii) Why is this information meaningless in this case?

## Section B

1 (a) Copy and complete this table and draw the graph of $y = x^2 - 5$ for $^-3 \le x \le 3$.

| $x$ | $^-3$ | $^-2$ | $^-1$ | 0 | 1 | 2 | 3 |
|---|---|---|---|---|---|---|---|
| $x^2$ | | 4 | | | | | 9 |
| $y = x^2 - 5$ | | $^-1$ | | | | | 4 |

(b) What is the equation of the line of symmetry of this graph?

(c) Use the graph to solve $x^2 - 5 = 0$.

2 (a) Copy and complete this table and draw the graph of $y = 3x^2 + 2$ for $^-3 \le x \le 3$.

| $x$ | $^-3$ | $^-2$ | $^-1$ | 0 | 1 | 2 | 3 |
|---|---|---|---|---|---|---|---|
| $x^2$ | | 4 | | | | | 9 |
| $3x^2$ | | 12 | | | | | 27 |
| $y = 3x^2 + 2$ | | 14 | | | | | 29 |

(b) What is the equation of the line of symmetry of this graph?

(c) What is the minimum value of $y$ for this graph?
How can you be sure that your answer is right without plotting more points?

(d) Use the graph to solve $3x^2 + 2 = 5$.

(e) Use the graph to solve $3x^2 + 2 = 11$ to one decimal place.

(f) Explain why there is no solution to $3x^2 + 2 = 0$.

## Section C

1 Write down the values of $x$ where the graph of each of these functions crosses the $x$-axis.
(You do not need to draw the graphs.)

(a) $y = (x + 5)(x + 1)$

(b) $y = (x - 3)(x + 2)$

(c) $y = (x - 7)(x + 3)$

(d) $y = (x - 3)(x + 4)$

2 For the function $y = x(x + 4)$ …

(a) What two values of $x$ make $x(x + 4) = 0$?

(b) Write down the coordinates of the points where $y = x(x + 4)$ crosses the $x$-axis.

3 For each of the following functions …
• Factorise the right-hand side.
• Write down the values of $x$ where the graph of the function crosses the $x$-axis.

(a) $y = x^2 + 5x + 4$

(b) $y = x^2 - 7x$

(c) $y = x^2 + 4x + 4$

(d) $y = x^2 - 3x - 4$

(e) $y = x^2 - 4$

(f) $y = x^2 + x - 12$

**4** The diagram shows the graphs of
$y = x^2 + 2x + 1$, $y = x^2 + 4x - 1$
and $y = x^2 - 4x + 4$.

(a) By substituting $x = 0$
(or any other value of $x$) into each
equation, work out which graph
corresponds to each equation.

(b) Write down the solutions to each of
these equations.

(i) $x^2 + 2x + 1 = 0$

(ii) $x^2 + 4x - 1 = 0$

(iii) $x^2 - 4x + 4 = 0$

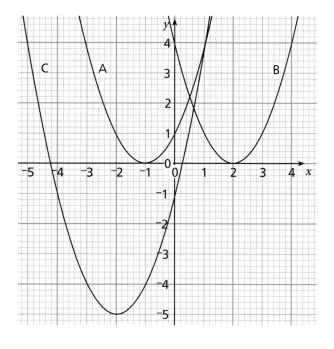

## Section D

**1** Sophie has 60 m of lawn edging.
She wishes to use it to edge a rectangular lawn as in the diagram.

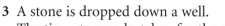

(a) Write down an expression for the area, $A$, of the lawn, in m².

(b) Plot the graph of $A$ for values of $x$ between 0 and 30.

(c) For what values of $x$ is the area 80 m²?

(d) What values of $x$ give an enclosed area greater than 210 m²?

(e) What is the maximum area lawn that Sophie can make?

(f) What are the lengths of the sides for this maximum area?

**2** Students are asked to make an open-topped box which must be 1 cm deep.
The perimeter of the base of the box must be 12 cm.

(a) Write down an expression for the volume, $V$ cm³,
of the box in terms of the width, $x$ cm.

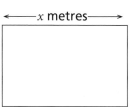

(b) Plot the graph of $V$ for values of $x$ between 0 and 6.

(c) For what values of $x$ is the volume greater than 6 cm³?

(d) For what value of $x$ is $V$ maximum?

**3** A stone is dropped down a well.
The time, $t$ seconds, taken for the stone to hit the water is recorded.
The equation $d = 5t^2$ is used to work out the depth of the well, $d$ metres.

(a) Draw up a table of suitable values of $t$ and $d$.

(b) Use the table to graph the function.

(c) If a splash is heard after 3.5 seconds, use your graph to estimate the depth of the well.
Check your answer by calculation.

## Section E

1 On a sheet of 2 mm graph paper draw axes with $^-2 \leq x \leq 2$ and $^-6 \leq y \leq 10$.

(a) Plot the graph of $y = 3x^2 - 5$.

(b) Draw and label suitable lines to solve these equations.
Label each line clearly with its equation.
Give solutions to one decimal place.

  (i) $3x^2 - 5 = 0$     (ii) $3x^2 - 5 = x$     (iii) $3x^2 - 5 = 2x$

2 (a) Copy and complete this working to
rearrange the equation $3x^2 - x - 6 = 0$
into the form $3x^2 - 5 = \ldots$

  $$3x^2 - x - 6 = 0$$
  $$3x^2 - 6 = \blacklozenge$$
  $$3x^2 - 5 = \blacklozenge$$

(b) On a sheet of 2 mm graph paper draw
axes with $^-2 \leq x \leq 2$ and $^-6 \leq y \leq 8$ and plot the graph of $y = 3x^2 - 5$.

(c) Draw and label a suitable line to solve the equation $3x^2 - x - 6 = 0$.
Write down the solutions to one decimal place.

3 (a) Rearrange the equation $3x^2 - x - 3 = 0$ into the form $3x^2 - 5 = \ldots$

(b) Working on the same axes as used for question 2, draw a suitable line to
solve the equation $3x^2 - x - 3 = 0$, giving answers to one decimal place.

4 (a) On a sheet of 2 mm graph paper draw axes with $^-2 \leq x \leq 2$ and $^-6 \leq y \leq 16$ and
plot the graph of $y = 4x^2 - 2$.

(b) Rearrange the equation $4x^2 - x - 6 = 0$ into the form $4x^2 - 2 = \ldots$

(c) Draw a suitable line to solve the equation $4x^2 - x - 6 = 0$,
giving answers to one decimal place.

(d) Rearrange the equation $4x^2 + x - 10 = 0$ into the form $4x^2 - 2 = \ldots$

(e) Working on the same axes as used for parts (a) and (c), draw a suitable line to
solve the equation $4x^2 + x - 10 = 0$.

5 (a) On a sheet of 2 mm graph paper draw axes with $^-3 \leq x \leq 3$ and $^-4 \leq y \leq 16$ and
plot the graph of $y = 15 - 2x^2$.

(b) Rearrange the equation $5 - 2x^2 - 2x = 0$ into the form $15 - 2x^2 = \ldots$

(c) Draw a suitable line to solve the equation $5 - 2x^2 - 2x = 0$,
giving answers to one decimal place.

(d) Working on the same axes as used for parts (a) and (c) draw a suitable line to
solve the equation $3 - 2x^2 - x = 0$.

**6** Suppose you are given the graph of $y = 6x^2 - 4$.

- Rearrange each equation below into the form $6x^2 - 4 = \ldots$
- Write down the equation of the line you would draw to solve the equation.

You **do not need** to draw the lines or solve the equations.

(a) $6x^2 = x + 2$        (b) $6x^2 - 2x = 4$

(c) $6x^2 - x + 6 = 0$        (d) $6x^2 - 4x - 2 = 0$

**7** If you are given the graph of $y = 2x^2 + 3x,$ what line would you need to draw to solve each of these equations?

(a) $2x^2 + 3x = 5$        (b) $2x^2 + 3x - 8 = 0$

(c) $2x^2 + 4x - 1 = 0$        (d) $2x^2 + 6x - 4 = 0$

**8** (a) Copy and complete the table of values for $y = x^2 - 2x - 4$ for $^{-}3 \leq x \leq 5$.

| $x$ | $^{-}3$ | $^{-}2$ | $^{-}1$ | 0 | 1 | 2 | 3 | 4 | 5 |
|---|---|---|---|---|---|---|---|---|---|
| $x^2$ | | | 1 | | | | 9 | | |
| $^{-}2x$ | | | 2 | | | | $^{-}6$ | | |
| $^{-}4$ | | | $^{-}4$ | | | | $^{-}4$ | | |
| $y$ | | | $^{-}1$ | | | | $^{-}1$ | | |

(b) On a sheet of $2\,\text{mm}$ graph paper draw axes with $^{-}3 \leq x \leq 5$ and $^{-}6 \leq y \leq 12$ and draw the graph of $y = x^2 - 2x - 4$.

(c) (i) Use your graph to solve the equation $x^2 - 2x - 4 = 10$.

(ii) Use your graph to solve the equation $x^2 - 2x - 4 = x$.

(iii) Use your graph to solve the equation $x^2 - 2x - 4 = 0$.

(iv) What happens if you try to solve the equation $x^2 - 2x - 4 = ^{-}5$?
What can you say about the equation $x^2 - 2x - 4 = ^{-}5$?

(d) The graph of $y = x^2 - 2x - 4$ and a graph of the form $y = mx + c$ can be used to solve the equation $x^2 - 4x - 5 = 0$.
Find the values of $m$ and $c$ needed and draw the line to find the solutions.

**9** (a) Copy and complete this working to rearrange the equation $4x^2 + 8x - 5 = 0$ into the form $2x^2 + 2x = \ldots$

(b) What line would you draw on the graph of $y = 2x^2 + 2x$ to solve the equation $4x^2 + 8x - 5 = 0$?

> $4x^2 + 8x - 5 = 0$
>
> $2x^2 + 4x - \clubsuit = 0$
>
> $2x^2 + 2x = \clubsuit - \clubsuit x$

**\*10** Work out what line you would draw on the graph of $y = 2x^2 + 2x$ to solve the equation $6x^2 + 9x - 6 = 0$.

# Mixed questions 6

**1** A is the point $(0, 4)$.
The equation of graph $a$ is $y = x^2$.

What are the equations of the other graphs?

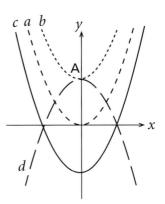

**2** A child's toy consists of a cone, a cylinder and a hemisphere joined together as shown.

(a) Calculate the total volume of the toy.
Show all your working carefully.
Give your answer to an appropriate degree of accuracy.

(b) Do the same for the total surface area of the toy.

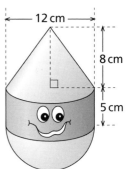

**3** ABCD is a square whose diagonals intersect at E.
Triangle ABE can be mapped on to triangle ACD by a rotation followed by an enlargement.
Describe each of these two transformations fully.

**4** Karen is playing Bingo. 50 balls numbered 1 to 50 are put into a box, drawn one by one at random and called out.
Each player has a card with eight different numbers in the range 1 to 50.
What is the probability that the first two numbers called out are on Karen's card?

**5** Factorise these expressions fully.

(a) $12a^2b + 8ab$          (b) $x^2 - 81$          (c) $x^2 - 7x - 18$

**6** This diagram shows the graph of the function $y = 7x - x^2$.

(a) Find the coordinates of point A.

(b) Find the coordinates of point B.

(c) The $x$-coordinates of C and D can be found by solving the equation $7x - x^2 = 10$.
Rearrange this equation and solve it.

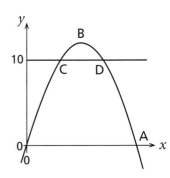

7 List the integer values of $n$ that satisfy the inequality $^{-}1 \leq \dfrac{3n+1}{2} < 4$.

8 (a) Find the equation of the line labelled $a$.

(b) Write down the three inequalities satisfied by points inside the shaded region (including the boundaries).

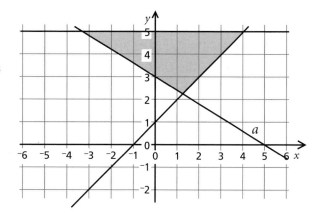

9 A population of $3.76 \times 10^9$ is expected to increase by 2.5% each year. What is the expected population after two years?

⊠ 10 (a) Write 840 as a product of prime numbers.

(b) A rectangular hall measures 8.4 m by 11 m.
What is the size, in cm, of the largest square tile that could be used to tile the hall floor completely without having to cut any tiles?

11 A road which runs in the direction from SW to NE goes through a village V.
A farm F is situated 15 km from V on a bearing of 070° from V.

(a) Calculate how far east the farm is from the village (the distance FG in the diagram).

(b) Calculate how far east the farm is from the road (the distance FH in the diagram).

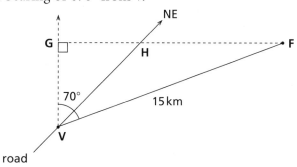

⊠ 12 This bar chart shows the times taken by a group of people to complete a puzzle.

(a) How many people are in the group?

(b) Calculate an estimate of the mean time taken.

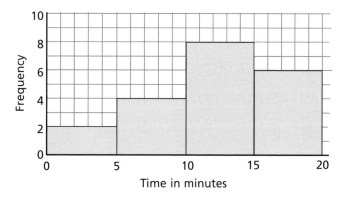

**13** Draw accurately triangle PQR with PQ = 5 cm, QR = 8 cm and RP = 10 cm.
Shade the locus of points in the triangle that are closer to PQ than to QR
and are also closer to Q than to P.

**14** The fuel consumption of a van is 13.6 litres per 100 km.

    (a) Calculate the amount of fuel the van uses to travel 450 km.

    (b) Calculate the distance that the van can travel on 66 litres of fuel.

**15** The square and the triangle have equal areas.
Find the possible values of $a$.

**16** A cone has base radius 7 cm and curved surface area 200 cm².

    (a) Find the slant height of the cone.

    (b) Find the volume of the cone.

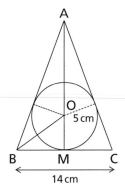

**17** A line has equation $3x + 5y = 2$.

    (a) Write down the gradient of the line.

    (b) Find the equation of the line perpendicular to $3x + 5y = 2$
    that passes through point (0, 2).

**18** In this diagram a circle of radius 5 cm with centre O
touches all three sides of an isosceles triangle ABC whose
base BC = 14 cm.
The circle touches the base at M.

    (a) Calculate angle OBM and hence angle ABM.

    (b) Calculate AM and hence the area of triangle ABC.

    (c) What percentage of the area of the triangle ABC
    is the area of the circle? Give your answer to the
    nearest 1%.

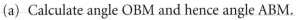

**\*19** In a class one quarter of the boys are left-handed.
One quarter of the left-handed pupils are girls.
Right-handed boys are three tenths of the class.

    What fraction of the class is right-handed girls?

**\*20** What fraction of the larger hexagon
is the area of the smaller one?

    Explain your answer.

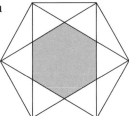

# 27 Algebraic fractions

## Section A

1 Find the value of each of the following when $p = \frac{1}{2}$ and $q = 4$.

   (a) $pq^2$           (b) $q - \frac{1}{p}$         (c) $p^2q$         (d) $(pq)^2$

   (e) $\frac{1}{p^2}$           (f) $p^2q^3$          (g) $\frac{1}{pq}$          (h) $\frac{q}{p}$

2 Find the value of each of the following when $m = \frac{3}{4}$ and $n = {}^-3$.

   (a) $\frac{m}{n} - \frac{n}{m}$           (b) $2n^2$               (c) $\frac{m^2}{n}$

3 If $a = 2$, $b = 3$ and $c = \frac{2}{5}$ calculate the following, leaving your answers as fractions.

   (a) $a^{-1}$      (b) $b^{-2}$      (c) $\left(\frac{a}{b}\right)^{-1}$     (d) $c^{-1}$      (e) $\left(\frac{c}{a}\right)^{-2}$

4 Simplify these.

   (a) $p^2 \times p^3$       (b) $m^5 \div m^3$      (c) $a^6 \times a^{-3}$     (d) $\frac{a^2 \times a^4}{a^3}$

5 Simplify these.

   (a) $\frac{a^3b}{a}$         (b) $\frac{a^2b^3}{ab}$       (c) $\frac{a^4b^3}{a^2b}$      (d) $\frac{(ab^2)^3}{ab}$

6 Simplify these.

   (a) $\frac{6m^2n}{3n}$       (b) $2m^3 \times 5mn^2$   (c) $(4m^2n^3)^{-3}$    (d) $\frac{8m^5n^3}{(2m^2)^2}$

7 Simplify these as far as possible.

   (a) $\frac{ab^2}{a^2} \times ab$    (b) $\frac{x^2y^4}{x} \times x^{-3}$   (c) $\frac{x^5y^3}{x^2y^4} \times x^3y^{-2}$   (d) $\frac{x^3y}{y^2} \times x^{-2}y^{-1}$

## Section B

1 Find the value of each of these.

   (a) $\sqrt{49 \times 16}$   (b) $4 \times \sqrt{64}$     (c) $\sqrt{3600}$     (d) $\sqrt{3^4 \times 2^2}$

2 Find the value of each of these.

   (a) $\sqrt{\frac{4^2}{2^2}}$       (b) $\sqrt{\frac{25 \times 49}{36}}$   (c) $\sqrt{\frac{5^4}{3^6}}$     (d) $\sqrt{\frac{4^8}{5^4}}$

3 Simplify these.

   (a) $\sqrt{16a^2}$      (b) $\sqrt{144a^4b^2}$   (c) $\sqrt{a^6b^4c^8}$    (d) $\sqrt{\frac{a^{10}}{16}}$

4 Simplify these.

   (a) $\sqrt{a^{-4}}$      (b) $\sqrt{a^{-2}b^6}$   (c) $\sqrt{\frac{81a^4}{a^6}}$    (d) $\sqrt{\frac{121a^8}{a^2}}$

5 Simplify these.

   (a) $a^3b^2 \times \sqrt{\frac{a^4}{b^6}}$   (b) $a^{-2}b^2 \times \sqrt{\frac{a^4}{b^2}}$   (c) $\sqrt{\frac{a^6}{b^8}} \times \sqrt{b^{-6}}$   (d) $\sqrt{a^{-4}b^2} \times \sqrt{\frac{a^6}{b^4}}$

## Section C

1  Multiply out each of these expressions.
   (a)  $3(2x - 5)$      (b)  $4x(x + 5)$      (c)  $\frac{1}{3}ab(6a + 9)$      (d)  $\frac{1}{2}a^2b(8b - 2ab)$

2  Simplify these.
   (a)  $\frac{5a^2 - 7a}{a}$      (b)  $\frac{24b^2 + 18b}{6b}$      (c)  $\frac{12ab - 16a}{4a}$      (d)  $\frac{21ab + 7a^2b}{7ab}$

3  Factorise these completely.
   (a)  $25a^2 + 15a$      (b)  $72ab^2 - 32a^2b$      (c)  $21a^3 + 14a^2$      (d)  $40a^2b^4 - 35a^3b^2$

4  Simplify these.
   (a)  $\frac{1}{d^2}(d^3 + d^5)$      (b)  $\frac{d^8 - d^3}{d^2}$      (c)  $d^{-3}(8d^5 + d^2)$      (d)  $(6d^4 - 8d^3) \div 2d^5$

5  Simplify these.
   (a)  $\frac{a^2b - a^2b^2}{ab}$      (b)  $\frac{a^2b^2 - a^3b}{a^2b^2}$      (c)  $\frac{12a^3b^2 - 3ab}{6a^2}$      (d)  $\frac{4a^4b^3 + 2ab^2}{8a^5b^5}$

## Section D

1  Write each of these as a single fraction.
   (a)  $\frac{2}{9} + \frac{3}{4}$      (b)  $\frac{a}{4} + \frac{a}{3}$      (c)  $\frac{4a}{3} - \frac{2a}{5}$      (d)  $\frac{3a}{6} + \frac{4a}{3}$

2  Write each of these as a single fraction.
   (a)  $\frac{1}{2a} + \frac{1}{3a}$      (b)  $\frac{2}{3a} - \frac{1}{2a}$      (c)  $\frac{6a}{5} - \frac{1}{3a}$      (d)  $\frac{1}{4a} + \frac{5a}{3}$

3  Write each of these as a single fraction and simplify it as far as possible.
   (a)  $\frac{a+1}{2} + \frac{a}{3}$      (b)  $\frac{2a+3}{6} + \frac{a}{3}$      (c)  $\frac{3a-2}{4} + \frac{3}{a}$      (d)  $\frac{5-4a}{6} + \frac{2}{3a}$

4  Write each of these as a single fraction and simplify it.
   (a)  $\frac{a+3}{2} + \frac{2a-1}{3}$      (b)  $\frac{a}{3} + \frac{a^2-4}{2a}$      (c)  $\frac{6a+3}{4} - \frac{3a+1}{5}$      (d)  $\frac{a+5}{3} + \frac{2a+1}{4} + \frac{a+3}{2}$

5  Simplify these.
   (a)  $1 + \frac{2a}{5}$      (b)  $2 + \frac{3a+1}{4}$      (c)  $6 - \frac{2a+4}{5}$      (d)  $7 - \frac{3a-2}{4}$

6  Simplify these.
   (a)  $\frac{3}{4} \times \frac{2}{3}$      (b)  $\frac{4a}{5} \times \frac{2}{3a}$      (c)  $\frac{3a^2}{4b} \times \frac{2b^2}{a}$      (d)  $\frac{2a+1}{a} \times \frac{3a}{4}$

7  Simplify these.
   (a)  $2 \div \frac{3}{4}$      (b)  $3 \div a^2$      (c)  $4a^2 \div \frac{1}{2}$      (d)  $\frac{1}{2a} \div a^2$

8  Simplify these.
   (a)  $\frac{2a^2}{3} \div \frac{1}{a}$      (b)  $\frac{3ab^2}{4} \div \frac{a}{b}$      (c)  $\frac{5ab}{3} \div \frac{10b}{a}$      (d)  $\frac{a^2 + 3b}{4a} \div \frac{a}{b}$

# 28 Further graphs

## Section A

1 (a) (i) Copy and complete the following table of values for $y = x^2 - 3x$.

| $x$ | $^-2$ | $^-1$ | 0 | 1 | 2 | 3 | 4 | 5 |
|---|---|---|---|---|---|---|---|---|
| $x^2 - 3x$ | | 4 | | | $^-2$ | | | |

    (ii) Use the values from your table to plot the graph of $y = x^2 - 3x$.

    (iii) Use your graph to solve the equation $x^2 - 3x = 4$.

  (b) (i) Copy and complete this table for $y = x^3 + 2$ for values of $x$ between $^-2$ and 2.

| $x$ | $^-2$ | $^-1$ | 0 | 1 | 2 |
|---|---|---|---|---|---|
| $x^3 + 2$ | | 1 | | | 10 |

    (ii) Use your values to plot the graph of $y = x^3 + 2$
        on the same axes you used for part (a).

    (iii) Use your second graph to solve the equation $x^3 + 2 = 0$.
        Check your answer by an algebraic method.

  (c) Use both your graphs to solve the equation $x^2 - 3x = x^3 + 2$.
     If you have access to a graphical calculator, use the TRACE function to
     check your answer.

  (d) Describe the symmetries of each of the two graphs.

2 (a) Copy and complete the following table of values,
     adding extra lines if you wish, for $y = x^3 + x^2 - 3x$.

| $x$ | $^-3$ | $^-2$ | $^-1$ | 0 | 1 | 2 |
|---|---|---|---|---|---|---|
| $x^3 + x^2 - 3x$ | | 2 | | | $^-1$ | |

  (b) Plot the graph of $y = x^3 + x^2 - 3x$ using the values from your table.

  (c) Solve the equation $x^3 + x^2 - 3x = 6$ and explain your method of solution.

  (d) Rearrange the equation $x^3 + x^2 - 5x = 1$ so that you can solve it by using your graph
     together with a suitable straight line. Solve this equation.

3 (a) Draw up a table of values for $y = 5 - x^3$ and for $y = 2x^2 - 4x + 3$
     for values of $x$ from $^-1$ to 2.
     Draw suitable axes and plot the graphs on these axes.

  (b) Estimate the value of $x$ which makes $2x^2 - 4x + 3$ a minimum.
     What is this minimum value?

  (c) What are the values of $x$ at the points where the two graphs intersect?
     Write down an equation which has these $x$-values as its solutions.

**4** (a) Plot the graphs of $y = x^3 + 2x^2 - 7$ and $y = 2x^2 - 5x$ for values of $x$ between $^-2$ and 3 on suitable axes.

  (b) Use your graphs to find a solution of the equation $x^3 + 5x = 7$.

  (c) Use trial and improvement to check your solution to two decimal places.

You do not need to draw any graphs for questions 5 or 6.

**5** Explain how you could use the graph of $y = x^3 - 6x^2$ to solve each of the following equations, giving the equations of any additional lines you would need to draw.

  (a) $x^3 - 6x^2 = 5$          (b) $x^3 - 6x^2 = 3x - 2$

  (c) $x^3 - 6x^2 - 2x = 0$      (d) $5 + x^3 = 6x^2$

**6** The curved graph shown has equation $y = x^3 - 3x^2 + 3$.

  (a) Describe the symmetry of the graph of $y = x^3 - 3x^2 + 3$.

  (b) Select one of the three straight lines P, Q or R and use it to solve $x^3 - 3x^2 = 2x$.

  (c) The equation $x^3 - 3x^2 + 3 = k$ has three solutions ($k$ is a constant). What is the range of possible values for $k$?

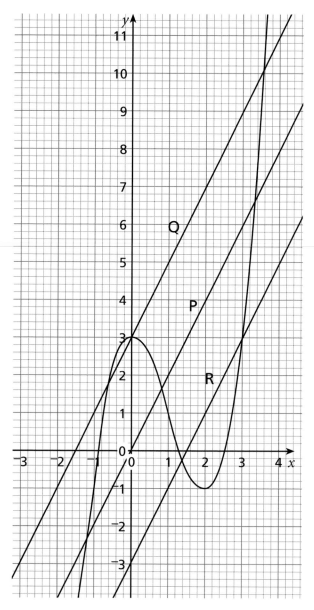

## Section B

1 Taking values of $x$ from $^-4$ to 4, plot on the same axes
  the graphs of $y = \frac{1}{x}$ and $y = x + 1$.

  (a) Describe the symmetries of the graph of $y = \frac{1}{x}$.

  (b) Which of the following equations are equivalent to $y = \frac{1}{x}$?

      (i) $xy = 1$      (ii) $xy - 1 = 0$      (iii) $1 - xy = 0$

      (iv) $x = \frac{1}{y}$      (v) $x + y = 1$

  (c) Use your graphs to solve the equation $\frac{1}{y} = x + 1$.

      Use a graphical calculator or graphing software to check your answer.

2 On another pair of axes, and taking values of $x$ from $^-6$ to 6,
  draw the graphs of $y = \frac{12}{x}$ and $y = 3x$.

  (a) Describe the symmetry of the graph of $y = \frac{12}{x}$.

  (b) Use your graphs to find the solutions to $\frac{12}{x} = 3x$.
      Check your answer algebraically.

*3 On new axes, with $^-3 \le x \le 3$, draw the graphs of $y = 10 - \frac{6}{x}$ and $y = x^2$.

  Use your graphs to solve the equation $x^2 + \frac{6}{x} = 10$.

## Section C

1 (a) Select four equations from the following list to match the sketch graphs below.

      A  $y = \frac{^-10}{x}$      B  $y = x^2 + 3$      C  $y = 5 - x^2$

      D  $y = 3x + 1$      E  $y = x^3 - 1$      F  $y = x^2 + x$

  (i) 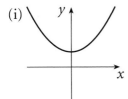    (ii) 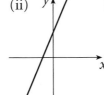    (iii) 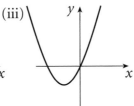    (iv)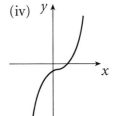

  (b) Sketch a graph for each of the two remaining equations.

**2** (a) Match the following equations to four of the sketch graphs below.

(i) $y = \frac{1}{x}$ (ii) $y = x^2$ (iii) $y = {}^-x^2$ (iv) $y = {}^-x^3$

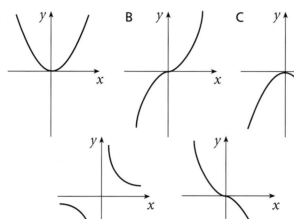

(b) Suggest equations for the two remaining sketch graphs.

## Section D

**1** 200 metres of fencing is to be used to make three sides of a rectangular camping site running alongside a river.

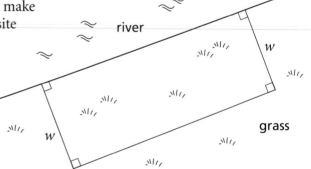

The width of the site is $w$ metres.

(a) Show that the area, $A\,\text{m}^2$, of the site is given by $A = w(200 - 2w)$.

(b) What is the greatest value that $w$ could take?

(c) Make a table of values for $A$ and $w$.
    Plot the graph of $A = w(200 - 2w)$.

(d) Use your graph to estimate the value of $w$ for which $A = 4000$.
    Give the length and width of the site for this value of $A$.

(e) Find the value of $w$ for which the greatest possible area can be enclosed by the 200 m fencing. What is this greatest area?

**2** A small, open gift box is to be made from a piece of metallic finish card measuring 16 cm by 20 cm.
A square with edge length $s$ cm is to be cut from each corner and the remaining rectangular sections along each edge are to be folded up to make the box shape, as shown.

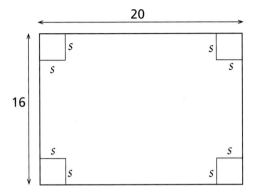 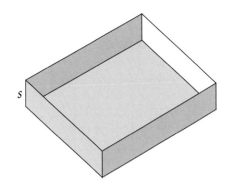

(a) What are the dimensions of the base of the gift box in terms of $s$?

(b) Find an expression for the capacity, $C$, of the box.
Explain how you can tell whether this is a quadratic or cubic function of $s$.

(c) Plot a graph to show how the capacity, $C$ cm$^3$, of the box varies with the length, $s$ cm, of the sides of the squares cut from the corners.
Describe how the shape of the graph relates to your last answer about whether this function is quadratic or cubic.

(d) (i) Find the value of $s$ which makes the box have the largest possible capacity.

(ii) The volume of a large tube of chocolate beans is 400 cm$^3$.
Explain, with reasons, whether you think the beans would fit in this gift box.

### Section B

1 Find the angles marked
with letters.
Explain how you worked
out each one.
O is the centre of each circle.

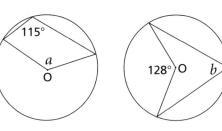

2 C is the centre of the circle.
Calculate angle ABD, giving a
reason for each step of working.

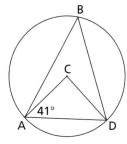

3 C is the centre of the circle.
Calculate angle ACB, giving a
reason for each step of working.

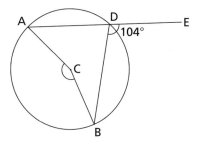

4 Calculate angles BCE and ADC,
giving reasons for each step
of working.

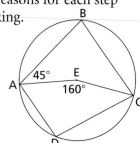

5 Calculate angle ADB,
giving reasons for each
step of working.

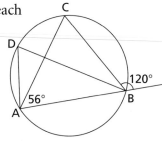

6 C is the centre of the circle.
Calculate angle EAD, giving a
reason for each step of working.

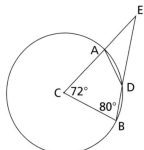

7 In the diagram
BC is parallel to AD.

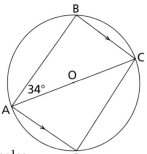

(a) Calculate these angles.
  (i) ABC  (ii) ACB  (iii) ADC  (iv) CAD
(b) Comment on the line BD.
(c) What shape is ABCD?

## Section C

Give a reason for each step of working in these questions.

**1** Calculate the angles marked $x$ and $y$.

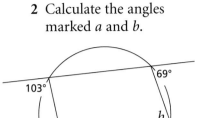

**2** Calculate the angles marked $a$ and $b$.

**3** In this diagram, PQ = PR. Calculate angle PSR.

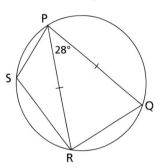

**4** Calculate angle AFE.

**5** Calculate angle PTS.

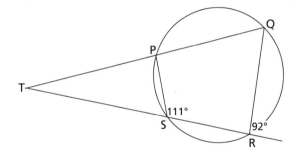

## Sections D and E

Give a reason for each step of working in these questions.

**1** Find angle ACB.

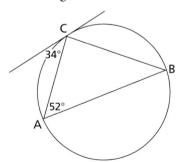

**2** AC is a diameter. Find angle ABC.

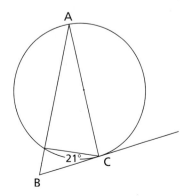

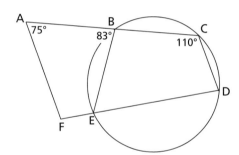

**3** Find angle PQS.

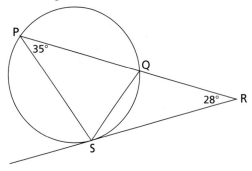

**4** Find these angles. (a) SPQ (b) SPU

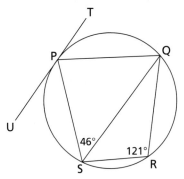

**5** Find angle JLK.

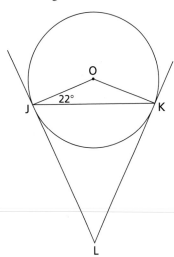

**6** Find the angle CAD.

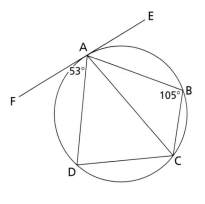

**7** Calculate angle ADB.

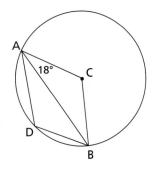

**8** Calculate angle YTZ.

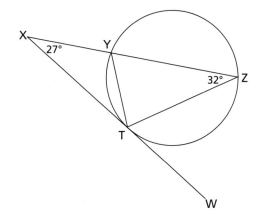

## Sections A and B

**1** Make the bold letter the subject in each of these formulas.

(a) $r = 5s + 6$      (b) $a = 2 + 7\mathbf{b}$      (c) $4b = 3\mathbf{c} - 5$

(d) $t = 5 - 3\mathbf{s}$      (e) $4y = 5 + 4\mathbf{s}$      (f) $p = 2a + 3\mathbf{f}$

**2** Which of these is a correct rearrangement of $p = 4q - 3r$?

A   $q = p + 3r - 4$      B   $r = \dfrac{p - 4q}{3}$      C   $q = \dfrac{p + 3r}{4}$

**3** Make the bold letter the subject in each of these formulas.

(a) $a = 7 + \dfrac{\mathbf{x}}{3}$      (b) $\dfrac{\mathbf{b} + 4}{6} = d$      (c) $p = \dfrac{5\mathbf{x}}{2} - 4$

**4** Make $x$ the subject of these formulas.

(a) $y = 2x - z$      (b) $a = db - fx$      (c) $p = 3(x + c)$

(d) $q(x + 5) = r$      (e) $3(a - x) = 4y$      (f) $5(x + 3) = 3y$

**5** Rearrange the following to make the bold letter the subject.

(a) $y = \dfrac{3\mathbf{x}}{z}$      (b) $f = 2 + \dfrac{g}{\mathbf{h}}$      (c) $p = \dfrac{q}{\mathbf{r}} - 7$

(d) $a = \dfrac{b}{\mathbf{d}} - c$      (e) $p = q - \dfrac{r}{\mathbf{t}}$      (f) $s = \dfrac{t + u}{\mathbf{v}}$

**6** Which of these are correct rearrangements of $p = \dfrac{q - t}{r}$?

A   $q = rp + t$      B   $t = r(p - q)$      C   $t = q - pr$

**7** Make the bold letter the subject.

(a) $s = \dfrac{t}{\mathbf{v} + w}$      (b) $3p = \dfrac{4q}{r - \mathbf{s}}$      (c) $a = \dfrac{b + c}{d + \mathbf{e}}$

## Section C

**1** Which of these is a correct rearrangement of $s = at - ap$?

A   $a = \dfrac{s}{t + p}$      B   $a = \dfrac{s}{t - p}$      C   $a = \dfrac{s}{p - t}$

**2** Make $x$ the subject of each of these.

(a) $y = bx + cx$      (b) $4x = ay - bx$      (c) $4x = by + dx$      (d) $ax + by = cx + dy$

**3** Make the letter in square brackets the subject of each of these.

(a) $pa = 4(a + q)$     $[a]$      (b) $r(p + q) = 6(p - q)$   $[q]$

(c) $st^2 - \dfrac{u(r + 3)}{s} = 0$     $[s]$      (d) $\dfrac{t^2 - 4s}{t} = tp$     $[t]$

(e) $a(x - y) = b(x + y)$   $[x]$      (f) $3(t + s) = r(3t - s)$   $[s]$

**4** Which of these is a correct arrangement of $a = \dfrac{4(b+c)}{bc}$ ?

A $\quad b = \dfrac{c}{ca-4}$  
B $\quad b = \dfrac{4c}{ca+4}$  
C $\quad c = \dfrac{4b}{ba-4}$  
D $\quad c = \dfrac{b}{ba+4}$  
E $\quad c = \dfrac{4b}{4-ba}$  
F $\quad b = \dfrac{4c}{ac-4}$

**5** From the expression $g = \dfrac{a+b}{a-b}$ write an expression for $a$ in terms of $b$ and $g$.

**6** (a) Make $t$ the subject of this formula: $s(t - u) = 3(t + u)$

 (b) Find the value of $t$ when $s = 5.64$ and $u = 1.56$.

## Section D

**1** This running track is formed from two rectangles and two semicircles.

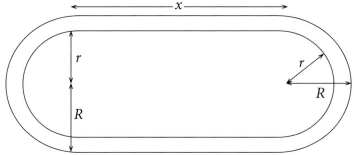

All measurements are in metres.

 (a) (i) If the length of the inside track is 400 m, show that $2\pi r + 2x = 400$.

  (ii) Make $r$ the subject of this equation.

  (iii) If $x = 80$ what is the value of $r$?  
   Give your answer correct to two decimal places.

  (iv) If the radius of the inside curve is 25 metres, what is the length  
   of the straight, to the nearest metre?

 (b) (i) Show that the area, $A\,\text{m}^2$, of the running track is given by  
   $$A = \pi R^2 - \pi r^2 + 2x(R - r).$$

  (ii) Find the area of the track when $R = 50$, $r = 30$ and $x = 80$.

  (iii) Make $x$ the subject of the formula.

  (iv) Calculate the value of $x$ when $A = 4000$, $R = 40$ and $r = 30$.

  (v) What is the length of the straight when the area is $3000\,\text{m}^2$  
   and the radii are 30 m and 25 m?

## Section E

1 Assume the Earth is a sphere of radius $6.35 \times 10^6$ metres.

   (a) Calculate the surface area of the Earth. Give your answer in standard form, to an appropriate degree of accuracy.

   (b) Rearrange the formula $A = 4\pi r^2$ to give $r$ in terms of $A$.

   (c) Venus is also roughly a sphere, and its surface area is $8.11 \times 10^{15}\,\text{m}^2$. Calculate the radius of Venus. Give your answer in standard form.

2 The surface area, $A$, of a cylinder with radius $r$ and height $h$ is given by the formula $A = 2\pi r^2 + 2\pi rh$.

   (a) Factorise the expression for $A$ fully.

   (b) Find the surface area of a cylinder with a radius of 2.3 metres and a height of 8.6 metres.
      Give your answer correct to one decimal place.

   (c) Make $h$ the subject of the formula.

   (d) Find the height of a cylinder with a radius of 6.4 cm and a surface area of 415.3 cm$^2$.

3 The volume of a pollen grain is $3.1 \times 10^{-5}\,\text{mm}^3$.
If it is roughly a sphere, calculate its radius.

4 The following formula gives the height, $h$, in terms of the initial velocity $u$, acceleration $a$ and time $t$.
$$h = ut + \tfrac{1}{2}at^2$$

   (a) Rewrite the formula to give $u$ in terms of $h$, $a$ and $t$.

   (b) Find the initial velocity if $a = {}^-9.8$ and the height is 56.1 when $t = 4$.

# Mixed questions 7

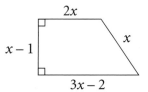

1 The diagram shows the dimensions of a trapezium. The perimeter of the trapezium is 32 cm.

Find the area of the trapezium.

2 A box of chocolates contains 8 milk chocolates and 4 dark chocolates. Alex takes two chocolates from the box at random.

Use a tree diagram to find the probability that he takes

(a) two dark chocolates

(b) at least one milk chocolate

3 (a) Simplify $\dfrac{6ab^2}{a^4} \times \dfrac{a^2 b}{2}$.
  (b) Simplify $\dfrac{2r^2 - rs^2}{r^2 s}$.

  (c) Write $\dfrac{a^2}{b} + \dfrac{b^2}{a}$ as a single fraction.
  (d) Write $\dfrac{x+5}{4} - \dfrac{x}{6}$ as a single fraction.

4 (a) Draw axes with $x$ and $y$ from 0 to 12.
    Draw the graph of $xy = 12$ for $1 \le x \le 12$.

  (b) On the same axes, draw the graph of $3x + 4y = 36$.

  (c) Use the graphs to find the values of $x$ and $y$ which satisfy both of the equations $xy = 12$ and $3x + 4y = 36$.

5 Make $r$ the subject of each of these formulas.

  (a) $s = \dfrac{a + br}{c}$
  (b) $s = a + \dfrac{b}{r}$
  (c) $s = \dfrac{a + r}{r}$
  (d) $s = \dfrac{a + r}{b + r}$

6 A price of £24 is increased by 10% and then by 10% again. What is the new price?

7 A, B, C and D are four points on the circumference of a circle.
PA is a tangent to the circle at A and TD is a tangent to the circle at D.
AD is a diameter of the circle.
Angle PAB = 38° and angle TDC = 22°.

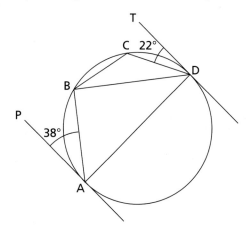

Calculate the following angles, giving reasons for your answers.

(a) Angle ABC

(b) Angle BCD

**8** Find the value of $2^1 - 2^0 + 2^{-1} - 2^{-2}$.

**9** Solve these equations.     (a) $r^2 + 7r = 0$          (b) $(t-6)(t+4) = 1 - 2t$

**10** $Q$ is directly proportional to $\sqrt{P}$.
When $P = 25$, $Q = 30$.

(a) Find the equation connecting $Q$ and $P$.

(b) Find    (i) the value of $Q$ when $P = 9$       (ii) the value of $P$ when $Q = 60$

**11** This table shows the age and gender distribution of the employees in a company.

| Age | 16–20 | 21–30 | 31–45 | 46–65 |
|---|---|---|---|---|
| Males | 28 | 35 | 47 | 42 |
| Females | 19 | 41 | 38 | 30 |

Mary is carrying out a survey about employee satisfaction in the company.
She wants to take a stratified sample of 50 employees from the whole company.

Calculate how many in the sample should be

(a) males aged 16–20

(b) females aged 31–45

(c) aged 46–65

**12** (a) Copy the grid and triangle ABC.

(b) Rotate triangle ABC 90° clockwise about (1, 1).
Label this triangle A′B′C′.

(c) Rotate triangle A′B′C′ 90° anticlockwise
about (0, ⁻1). Label this triangle A″B″C″.

(d) Describe fully the single transformation which
maps triangle ABC on to triangle A″B″C″.

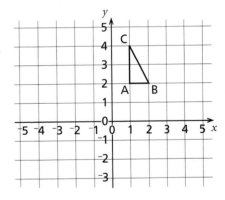

**13** The diagram shows a circle, centre O and radius 7 cm.
Angle ACB = 26°. DOB is a diameter of the circle.

Calculate the length of chord AB.

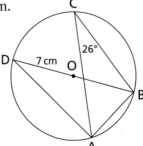

**\*14** The points A (9, 4), B (11, ⁻2) and C (⁻1, 4) all lie on a circle.
Find the coordinates of the centre of the circle.

# 31 Accuracy

## Section B

1 What are the upper and lower bounds of all the numbers for which
   (a) 6.4 is the nearest tenth
   (b) 0.1 is the nearest tenth
   (c) 50 is the nearest whole number
   (d) 250 is the nearest ten
   (e) 4.09 is the nearest hundredth

2 Write down the upper and lower bounds for each of these.
   (a) The length of a room is 2.8 m, correct to two significant figures.
   (b) The weight of a baby is 4.20 kg, correct to three significant figures.
   (c) The volume of a pond is 3.1 m$^3$, correct to two significant figures.
   (d) The length of a work surface is 1370 mm, correct to the nearest 10 mm.
   (e) The capacity of a jug is 350 ml, correct to the nearest 10 ml.
   (f) The weight of a parcel, to the nearest 100 g, is 1.5 kg.

## Section C

1 Find the upper and lower bounds of the total weight of three boxes each weighing 5.7 kg to the nearest 0.1 kg.

2 The dimensions of a room are measured as 3.7 m and 2.1 m, correct to two significant figures.
   Find the upper and lower bounds of
   (a) the perimeter of the room
   (b) the area of the room

3 Lara records the distances she cycles each day for a week.
   On five days she cycles 35 km and on two days she cycles 16 km.
   The distances are measured to the nearest kilometre.
   Find the upper and lower bounds of the distance she cycled during the week.

4 The dimensions of this trapezium are given to the nearest centimetre.
   Calculate the maximum possible area of the trapezium.

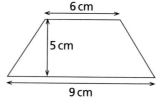

# Section D

1 A piece of wood is 1.6 m long, correct to the nearest 10 cm.
Jack cuts off a piece 72 cm long, correct to the nearest centimetre.
Find the upper and lower bounds of the length of wood remaining.

2 A partially empty tank has a total capacity of 2500 litres, to the nearest 10 litres.
To fill the tank, 1245 litres of oil, measured to the nearest litre, need to be added.
Find the upper and lower bounds of the original quantity of oil in the tank.

3 In this right-angled triangle, side $a = 4.7$ cm
and side $c = 5.4$ cm, both to the nearest 0.1 cm.

Calculate the upper and lower bounds for the side $b$.
Give each answer to four significant figures.

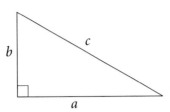

# Section E

1 The power dissipated in an electrical circuit is given by the formula
$$P = \frac{V^2}{R}$$
where $P$ is the power in watts, $V$ is the voltage and $R$ is the resistance in ohms.

Calculate the upper and lower bounds of the power if the voltage is 240 volts and
the resistance is 410 ohms, both measured to two significant figures.

2 A bottle of medicine contains 100 ml, correct to the nearest millilitre.
One dose of medicine is 5 ml.

If the doses are measured correct to the nearest millilitre, what is
the minimum number of doses in the bottle?

3 The population of England in 2000 was $50.0 \times 10^6$, correct to three significant figures.
The area of England is 130 000 km$^2$, correct to three significant figures.

Calculate the upper and lower bounds for the population density (people per km$^2$)
of England in 2000.
Give your answers correct to four significant figures.

*Similarity and enlargement*

## Section A

1  This shape is to be enlarged with scale factor 2.5.
   Make a sketch of the enlargement, showing its dimensions.

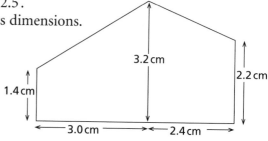

2  Shape P is enlarged with scale factor 2 to give shape Q.
   Shape Q is enlarged with scale factor 3 to give shape R.

   Give the scale factor of the enlargement

   (a)  from shape P to shape R

   (b)  from shape Q to shape P

   (c)  from shape R to shape Q

   (d)  from shape R to shape P

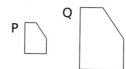

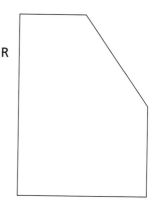

3  The scale factor of an enlargement from a shape A to a shape B is 1.4.
   The scale factor of an enlargement from B to a shape C is 1.25.

   (a)  What is the scale factor of the enlargement from A to C?

   (b)  What is the scale factor of the scaling from C to B?

## Section B

1  In each of these pairs of triangles, find the lengths labelled with letters.

   (a)

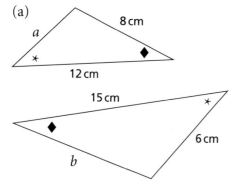

   (b)

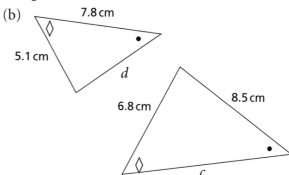

**2** In the diagram MN is parallel to JK.

(a) Explain why triangles JKL and MNL are similar.

(b) Find length MN.

(c) Find length KL.

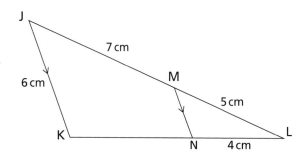

**3**

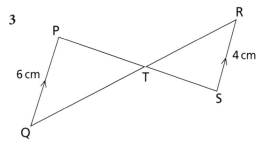

In the diagram PQ is parallel to RS.
PS = 12 cm.

(a) Prove that triangles PQT and SRT are similar.

(b) Find length TS.

**4** (a) Prove that triangles APY and BPX are similar.

(b) Find length AX.

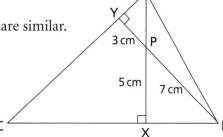

# Section C

**1** A standard photographic colour print is 150 mm by 100 mm.
Neil uses his scanner and computer to produce
an enlargement 390 mm by 260 mm.

(a) What is the scale factor of the enlargement?

(b) What is the area factor?

**2** This semicircle has an area of 12 cm².
Work out (i) the area factor
and (ii) the area of the enlarged shape
when the semicircle is enlarged with scale factor

(a) 5        (b) 2.2        (c) $\frac{5}{3}$        (d) 0.8

**3** What scale factor corresponds to each of these area factors?

(a) 4        (b) 1.69        (c) $2\frac{1}{4}$        (d) 8

**4** Two mirrors are of a similar shape.
The area of glass in the larger one is double that in the smaller.
The width of the larger mirror is 30 cm.

What is the width of the smaller mirror?

## Section D

**1** Sphere B has twice the diameter of sphere A.

(a) What is the area factor from the surface of A to the surface of B?

(b) What is the volume factor from A to B?

**2** Cuboids V and W are similar.
The scale factor from V to W is 1.1.

(a) What is the volume factor from V to W?

(b) Given that the volume of V is 2000 cm³,
what is the volume of W?

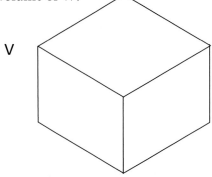

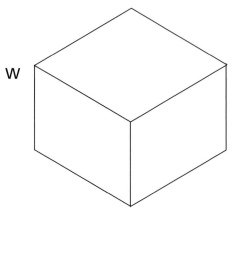

**3** Find the volume factor for an enlargement whose scale factor is

(a) 3       (b) 6       (c) 15       (d) 0.9       (e) 0.2

**4** These two glasses are similar.
The smaller glass holds 108 cm³ of liquid.
What does the larger one hold?

10 cm

6 cm

**5** Find the scale factor of an enlargement whose volume factor is

(a) 125       (b) 729       (c) 216 000       (d) 27 000       (e) 0.064

**6** These two bread tins are the same shape.
One is designed for a 1 pound loaf, the other for a 2 pound loaf.
What is the scale factor from the smaller one to the larger one?

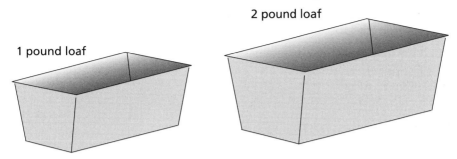

2 pound loaf

1 pound loaf

**7** Two tubes of toothpaste are the same shape but different sizes.
The large tube holds 350 g of toothpaste. The small tube holds 200 g.
The small tube is 12.0 cm long.
How long is the large tube?

**8** F and G are similar objects, made from the same material.
F's surface area is 6.25 times that of G.
The mass of G is 100 g. Find the mass of F.

**9** Three similar objects have surface areas in the ratio $4:25:49$.
Give the ratio of their volumes.

## Section E

**1** An architect draws a building to a scale of $1:50$.
A door is drawn 42 mm high and 18 mm wide.
How big **in metres** will the door be in real life?

**2** A plan of a room is drawn to a scale of $1:20$.
A large rug in the room has an area of $7 m^2$.
What area in $cm^2$ will this be represented by on the plan?

**3** A road contractor is working from a plan on a scale of $1:500$.
A stretch of road to be resurfaced covers $32.5 cm^2$ on the plan.
What is this area in $m^2$ on the real road?

**4** A model for a sculpture is made on a scale of $1:20$.
The model has a volume of $8000 cm^3$.
What will the volume of the finished sculpture be, in $m^3$?

# 34 Brackets and quadratic equations 2

## Section A

**1** Solve the following equations by factorising.

(a) $x^2 - 8x + 15 = 0$  (b) $x^2 + 10x + 21 = 0$  (c) $x^2 - 8x + 12 = 0$

(d) $x^2 - 3x - 10 = 0$  (e) $x^2 + 5x - 24 = 0$  (f) $x^2 - 7x = 0$

**2** Solve these equations by rearranging and factorising.

(a) $x^2 + 3x = 28$  (b) $x^2 = 13x - 22$  (c) $x^2 = 19x + 20$

(d) $x^2 = 20 - x$  (e) $x(x + 13) + 36 = 0$  (f) $x(x - 12) = 45$

**3** The area of this rectangle is $60\,\text{cm}^2$.

(a) Show that $x^2 + 3x - 88 = 0$.

(b) Solve the equation and hence
find the dimensions of the rectangle.

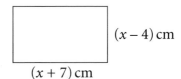
$(x - 4)\,\text{cm}$
$(x + 7)\,\text{cm}$

**4** The length of a rectangle is 8 cm more than its width, and its area is $240\,\text{cm}^2$.

(a) By letting the width of the rectangle be $x$, form an equation in $x$.

(b) Show that this equation can be simplified to become $x^2 + 8x - 240 = 0$.

(c) Solve the equation and hence find the dimensions of the rectangle.

**5** Bob's brother is 9 years older than he is. The product of their ages is 90.

(a) By letting $b$ stand for Bob's age, form an equation in $b$ and show that
it simplifies to become $b^2 + 9b - 90 = 0$.

(b) Solve this equation to find the ages of the brothers.

**6** The triangle and rectangle both have the same area.

(a) Form an equation in $x$ and show that
it simplifies to give $x^2 - 9x + 18 = 0$.

(b) Solve the equation and hence find the
two possible values for the area.

$(x - 1)\,\text{cm}$
$(x + 2)\,\text{cm}$

$(x - 2)\,\text{cm}$
$20\,\text{cm}$

## Section B

**1** Expand and simplify these expressions.

(a) $(2a + 3)(a + 2)$  (b) $(3b + 1)(2b - 3)$  (c) $(p - 5)(4p + 1)$

(d) $(6t - 5)(2t - 1)$  (e) $(r - 9)(2 + 5r)$  (f) $(4x + 1)(4x - 1)$

(g) $(4y + 3)(2 - y)$  (h) $(3t + 1)^2$  (i) $(5 - 2z)^2$

**2** Show that the difference in area between the large and small rectangles is $2x^2 + 14x + 5$.

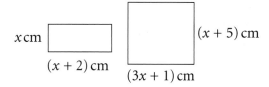

$x\,\mathrm{cm}$    $(x+2)\,\mathrm{cm}$    $(3x+1)\,\mathrm{cm}$    $(x+5)\,\mathrm{cm}$

**3** Copy and complete these.

(a) $(2x+3)(\quad) = 2x^2 + 7x + 6$    (b) $(\quad)(x-4) = 2x^2 - 11x + 12$

(c) $(3x-1)(\quad) = 6x^2 + 13x - 5$    (d) $(4x+3)(\quad) = 8x^2 - 6x - 9$

**4** Expand and simplify these where possible.

(a) $(x+5)(2y+1)$    (b) $(2x+y)(x-3y)$    (c) $(5y-2)(2x+y)$

(d) $(3x-2y)(x-y)$    (e) $(5x+y)^2$    (f) $(y-5)(x-3y)$

(g) $(4x-y)^2$    (h) $(5y-2x)^2$    (i) $(3x-2)(5x+4y)$

## Sections C and D

**1** Find pairs from the box that multiply to give

(a) $2x^2 + 5x + 2$    (b) $3x^2 + 5x - 2$

(c) $3x^2 - 5x - 2$    (d) $2x^2 - 3x - 2$

$$\boxed{\begin{array}{ll} (3x+1) & (3x-1) \\ (x+2) & (x-2) \\ (2x+1) & (2x-1) \end{array}}$$

**2** Factorise these.

(a) $2x^2 + 11x + 5$    (b) $3x^2 + 8x + 5$    (c) $3e^2 + 20e - 7$

(d) $7x^2 - 15x + 2$    (e) $5r^2 - 17r + 6$    (f) $2x^2 + 6x - 20$

(g) $3p^2 - 6p + 3$    (h) $4y^2 - 22y + 10$    (i) $35c^2 - 125c - 60$

**3** Factorise these.

(a) $4x^2 + 7x + 3$    (b) $4x^2 + 13x + 3$    (c) $6x^2 - 13x - 5$

(d) $8x^2 + 14x - 15$    (e) $20x^2 - 22x + 6$    (f) $120x^2 + 170x + 60$

**4** Factorise these.

(a) $p^2 - q^2$    (b) $x^2 - 25$    (c) $100y^2 - 1$    (d) $49a^2 - 4b^2$

**5** Which three of the following cannot be factorised using integers only?

A   $3a^2 + a - 2$    B   $3a^2 + a + 2$    C   $3a^2 - a - 2$

D   $3a^2 - a + 2$    E   $2a^2 - a + 3$    F   $2a^2 + a - 3$

**6** Solve these by factorising.

(a) $2x^2 - 15x + 7 = 0$    (b) $3x^2 - 5x - 2 = 0$    (c) $2x^2 + 9x + 9 = 0$

(d) $5x^2 - 7x + 2 = 0$    (e) $x^2 - 5x = 0$    (f) $3x^2 + 12x = 0$

(g) $4x^2 + 7x + 3 = 0$    (h) $4x^2 + 28x + 49 = 0$    (i) $2x^2 - 10x + 12 = 0$

(j) $12x^2 + 8x - 15 = 0$    (k) $9x^2 - 24x = 0$    (l) $24x^2 - 40x + 6 = 0$

**7** Solve the following quadratic equations by rearranging first.

(a) $2x^2 = x + 10$ 　　　　 (b) $5t^2 + 9t = 6 - 20t$ 　　　 (c) $6y^2 = 11y - 3$

(d) $12c^2 + 1 = 32c - 20$ 　　 (e) $10r = 25 - 8r^2$ 　　　　 (f) $4 - 10a = 10a - 9a^2$

**8** Factorise these.

(a) $10p^2 + 7pq + q^2$ 　　　 (b) $6r^2 - 7rs - 3s^2$ 　　　　 (c) $8c^2 - 11cd - 10d^2$

## Sections E and F

**1** Expand and simplify these perfect squares.

(a) $(x + 7)^2$ 　　　 (b) $(a - 2)^2$ 　　　 (c) $(c - 8)^2$ 　　　 (d) $(y + 9)^2$

**2** Copy and complete these.

(a) $(x - \blacksquare)^2 = x^2 - 12x + 36$ 　　　 (b) $(x + \blacksquare)^2 = x^2 + 30x + 225$

(c) $(x + \blacksquare)^2 = x^2 + 6x + \blacksquare$ 　　　 (d) $(x - \blacksquare)^2 = x^2 - 18x + \blacksquare$

**3** Which of the following expressions are perfect squares?

A　$x^2 - 2x + 1$ 　　　　　　　　 B　$x^2 + 4x - 4$

C　$x^2 - x + 1$ 　　　　　　　　 D　$x^2 - 4x + 4$

**4** Solve the following equations. Round to three decimal places where necessary.

(a) $(x + 2)^2 = 36$ 　　　 (b) $(x - 6)^2 = 49$ 　　　 (c) $(x - 1)^2 = 2$

**5** Solve the following equations by using perfect squares, giving each answer correct to three decimal places.

(a) $x^2 + 4x - 6 = 0$ 　　　 (b) $x^2 - 8x - 12 = 0$ 　　　 (c) $x^2 + 10x + 8 = 0$

(d) $x^2 + 2x - 13 = 0$ 　　　 (e) $x^2 + 14x + 3 = 0$ 　　　 (f) $x^2 - 20x + 15 = 0$

**6** (a) Expand and simplify $(x + \frac{9}{2})^2$.

(b) Hence solve the equation $x^2 + 9x - 4 = 0$.

**7** Solve the following equations by using perfect squares, giving each answer correct to three decimal places.

(a) $x^2 + 5x - 8 = 0$ 　　　　　　　 (b) $x^2 - 7x + 3 = 0$

**8** Solve these equations by first dividing, making 1 the coefficient of $x^2$.

(a) $2x^2 - 10x + 6 = 0$ 　　　　　　 (b) $4x^2 - 20x - 10 = 0$

(c) $2x^2 + 4x - 3 = 0$ 　　　　　　 (d) $5x^2 - 5x - 2 = 0$

## Section G

**1** Use the quadratic formula to solve each equation.

(a) $x^2 + 3x - 2 = 0$  (b) $x^2 - 6x + 2 = 0$  (c) $2x^2 - 5x + 3 = 0$

(d) $3x^2 + 4x - 8 = 0$  (e) $5x^2 + 7x + 2 = 0$  (f) $4x^2 - 2x - 7 = 0$

(g) $2x^2 - 5x = 8$  (h) $9x^2 = 12x + 4$  (i) $8x = x^2 + 5$

**2** Solve the following equations, choosing your own method each time.

(a) $x^2 - 7x + 12 = 0$  (b) $2x^2 + 13x - 7 = 0$  (c) $x^2 + 5x - 14 = 0$

(d) $x^2 + 8x - 3 = 0$  (e) $3x^2 + 2x - 1 = 0$  (f) $5x^2 - 3x - 4 = 0$

**3** (a) Solve the equation $2x^2 + 5x - 3 = 0$.

(b) Hence write down the coordinates of the points where the graph of $y = 2x^2 + 5x - 3$ crosses the x-axis.

**4** (a) Solve the equations if possible (one of them has no real solutions).

(i) $x^2 + 4x + 4 = 0$  (ii) $x^2 - 5x + 4 = 0$  (iii) $x^2 + 4x + 5 = 0$  (iv) $x^2 + 5x + 4 = 0$

(b) Use your solutions to the equations above to help you match each of the following equations with one of the graphs.

A  $y = x^2 + 4x + 4$    B  $y = x^2 - 5x + 4$    C  $y = x^2 + 4x + 5$    D  $y = x^2 + 5x + 4$

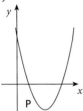
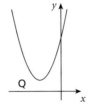
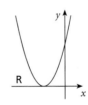
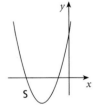

**5**

(2x + 3) cm

Rectangle A    2x cm

(x − 1) cm

Rectangle B    (x − 2) cm

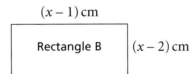

The area of rectangle A is 40 cm² greater than the area of rectangle B.

(a) Show that $x^2 + 3x - 14 = 0$.

(b) By solving the equation $x^2 + 3x - 14 = 0$, find the value of x correct to 3 d.p.

**6** Triangle ABC is right-angled.

The hypotenuse AC is 10 cm longer than the shortest side AB.
The product of these two lengths is 50.

Suppose x cm is the length of AB.

(a) Show that $x^2 + 10x - 50 = 0$.

(b) Solve this equation to find the length of the hypotenuse, correct to 2 d.p.

## Sections A–G: mixed questions

**1** Factorise these.

  (a) $4x^2 - 6x$         (b) $x^2 - 13x + 36$         (c) $2x^2 + x - 21$

**2** Solve these equations.

  (a) $x^2 - 2 = 7$         (b) $x^2 - 5x = 0$         (c) $x^2 + 2x = 24$

  (d) $(2x + 1)^2 = 25$      (e) $3x^2 + 16x - 35 = 0$     (f) $x^2 + 7x + 2 = 0$

  (g) $4x^2 + 9x = 0$       (h) $5x^2 - 2x - 4 = 0$

**3** The areas of these two rectangles are the same.

  (a) Show that $x^2 + x - 42 = 0$.

  (b) Solve this equation and
      hence find the area of each rectangle.

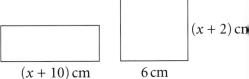

$(x - 3)\,\text{cm}$

$(x + 10)\,\text{cm}$       $6\,\text{cm}$

$(x + 2)\,\text{cm}$

**4** In this diagram, $PS = x\,\text{cm}$,
$QR = (x + 5)\,\text{cm}$ and angle $PSR = 90°$.

  The area of the triangle is $20\,\text{cm}^2$.

  (a) Show that $x^2 + 5x - 40 = 0$.

  (b) Solve the equation $x^2 + 5x - 40 = 0$.
      Hence find the length of QR, correct to 2 d.p.

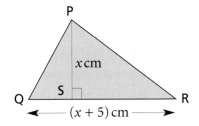

**5** A rectangular pond has a path on four sides as shown.

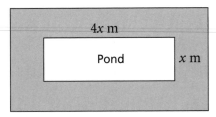

The pond has dimensions $x$ metres by $4x$ metres.
The path is 2 metres wide.

The total area of the pond and the path is $91\,\text{m}^2$.

  (a) Show that $4x^2 + 20x - 75 = 0$.

  (b) By solving the equation $4x^2 + 20x - 75 = 0$, find the area of the pond.

## Section H

1 Solve these pairs of simultaneous equations.

(a) $y = 10x - 16$
$y = x^2$

(b) $y = x^2 - 3$
$y = x + 9$

(c) $y = 2x^2 + x - 3$
$y = 2x$

2 Find the points of intersection for each pair of graphs.

(a)

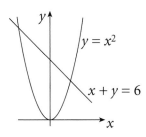

(b)

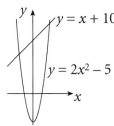

(c)

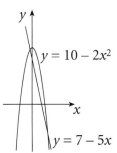

(d)

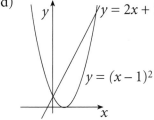

3 Match up the following pairs with the correct description, finding any points of intersection.

**A**
$y = x^2 - 2x$
$y = 4x - 9$

**B**
$y = 2x^2 + 1$
$y = 3x - 1$

**C**
$y = 2x^2 - 3x - 1$
$y = 2x + 2$

| The line crosses the curve twice. |

| The line and curve do not intersect. |

| The line just touches the curve. |

# Mixed questions 8

1 Expand and simplify the following.

   (a) $(x + 8)^2$        (b) $(y - 9)^2$        (c) $(a - b)^2$        (d) $(2c - d)^2$

2 Vinod has a picture that measures 8 cm by 10 cm.
He enlarges it so that it its area is twice as big.
What are the new dimensions of the picture?

3 The surface of a drive is to be a 10 cm layer of tarmac, measured to the nearest 1 cm.
The drive has been measured as 9 m long and 3.6 m wide, both to the nearest 10 cm.
Calculate the upper bound for the volume of tarmac required for the drive.

4 The letters $a$, $b$ and $h$ stand for lengths.
Which of the expressions on the right could represent

   (a) a length     (b) an area

   (c) a volume     (d) a pure number

$$\pi h \sqrt{a^2 + b^2}$$
$$\frac{a^2 h^2}{a + b} \qquad \frac{a^2 + b^2}{2h}$$
$$\frac{(a + b)^2}{2} \qquad \frac{a - b}{h}$$

5 Solve these quadratic equations, giving your answers to 2 d.p. where necessary.

   (a) $3x^2 + 4x - 15 = 0$        (b) $2x^2 + 13x = 24$        (c) $4x^2 = 3x + 9$

6 Mrs Jones invests £250 in a savings account for her grandson.
If the interest rate is 4% per annum, how much will be in the account after 10 years?

7 ABCD is a trapezium. Angles ABC and BCD are right angles.

   (a) Explain why triangles ABX and CDX are similar.

   (b) Find DC.

   (c) Find, correct to 1 d.p., the area of the trapezium.

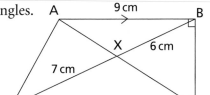

8 This table shows the amount spent on electricity each quarter by a household.

| Year | 1999 | 2000 | 2000 | 2000 | 2000 | 2001 | 2001 | 2001 |
|---|---|---|---|---|---|---|---|---|
| Quarter | 4 | 1 | 2 | 3 | 4 | 1 | 2 | 3 |
| Amount | £66 | £79 | £47 | £43 | £84 | £106 | £48 | £46 |

   (a) Calculate a 4-point moving average and show it with the original data on a graph.

   (b) Describe the trend.

**9** An advertiser has produced two different leaflets advertising a product.
They produce $7.5 \times 10^6$ copies of leaflet A and $4.3 \times 10^7$ copies of leaflet B.

If 3% of the copies of leaflet A are read and 0.8% of the copies of leaflet B are read, what percentage of all these leaflets are read?

**10** (a) Make a table of values for $y = x^3 - 3x$ for $^-3 \le x \le 3$.

(b) Draw the graph of $y = x^3 - 3x$ for $^-3 \le x \le 3$.

(c) Use your graph to solve the equation $x^3 - 3x - 10 = 0$.

(d) What is the equation of the straight line that you would need to draw to use the graph of $y = x^3 - 3x$ to solve the equation $x^3 - 5x - 1 = 0$?

(e) Draw the appropriate line and hence write down the solutions to $x^3 - 5x - 1 = 0$.

**11** Kirsty makes candles in the shape of square-based pyramids.
These two candles are similar.
The sloping edges have lengths 8 cm and 10 cm.

(a) The volume of the smaller candle is 96 cm³.
What is the volume of the larger candle?

(b) Kirsty makes another similar candle
that has a volume of 12 cm³.
Find the length of the sloping
edge of this candle.

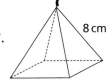
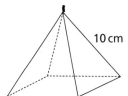

**12** Show algebraically that the line $y = 1 - x$ does not meet the curve $y = x^2 - 6x + 8$.

**13** A manufacturer makes a simple locking mechanism containing a spring and a lever.
The probability that the spring is faulty is 0.018 and, independently,
the probability that the lever is faulty is 0.004.

What is the probability that, in one locking mechanism,

(a) neither spring nor lever is faulty

(b) at least one of these two components is faulty

**14** (a) What must be added to the expression $x^2 - 10x$ to make it a perfect square?

(b) Use the perfect square to find, correct to 2 d.p., the solutions to the equations

(i) $x^2 - 10x = 5$       (ii)    $x^2 - 10x + 8 = 0$

**\*15** (a) Eva has four numbered cards face down on a table.
She turns over three of the cards and **adds** the numbers together.
The possible totals that she can get are 24, 27, 30 and 33.

What numbers are on Eva's cards?

(b) Mike also has four numbered cards.
He turns over three of the cards and **multiplies** the numbers together.
The possible products that he can get are 96, 180, 240 and 720.

What are the numbers on Mike's cards?

# 35 Trigonometric graphs

## Section A

1 Find these to the nearest 0.1° using a calculator.
  Give all the possible answers between $^-360°$ and 360°.

  (a) $\sin^{-1} 0.3$          (b) $\sin^{-1} {}^-0.65$          (c) $\sin^{-1} 0.8$

2 What angles between $^-720°$ and 720° have the same sine as each of these?

  (a) 45°         (b) $^-120°$         (c) 610°         (d) $^-500°$

3 Find all possible values of $x$ between 0° and 360° for each of these.

  (a) $3 \sin x = 0.6$     (b) $5 \sin x = 3$     (c) $\frac{1}{2} \sin x = 0.35$     (d) $2 \sin x + 3 = 4$

## Section B

1 Find these to the nearest 0.1° using a calculator.
  Give all possible answers between $^-360°$ and 360°.

  (a) $\cos^{-1} 0.8$          (b) $\cos^{-1} {}^-0.74$          (c) $\cos^{-1} {}^-0.3$

2 Find all possible values of $x$ between 0° and 360° for each of these.

  (a) $\cos x = 0.2$             (b) $3 \cos x - \frac{1}{4} = 0$

## Section C

1 Find all possible values of $x$ between 0° and 360° for each of these.

  (a) $\tan x = 3$       (b) $3 \tan x = {}^-1$       (c) $\cos x = \sin 30$

  (d) $2 \cos x = \tan 60$       (e) $\frac{1}{2} \tan x = \sin 60$       *(f) $\sin 2x = {}^-0.6$

## Section D

1 Sketch the following graphs, marking the key points.

  (a) $y = \frac{1}{2} \cos x$     (b) $y = \sin x + 3$     (c) $y = {}^-\sin x$     (d) $y = 2 \cos x - 1$

**2** Suggest an equation for each of these graphs.

(a)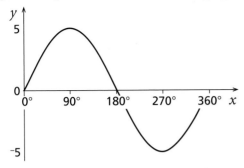

(b)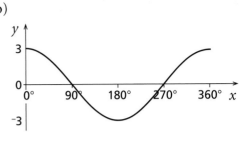

(c)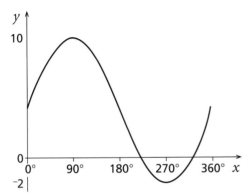

(d)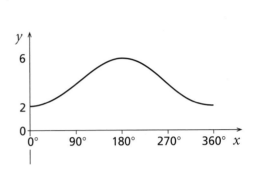

(e)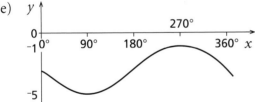

**3** Sketch the following graphs, marking the key points.

(a) $y = \sin(3x)$ (b) $y = 3\cos(2x)$ (c) $y = \sin(4x) + 2$ (d) $y = \cos\left(\frac{1}{2}x\right)$

**4** Suggest an equation for each of these graphs.

(a)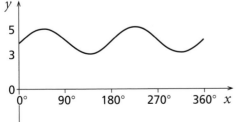

(b)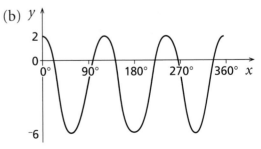

# 36 *Pattern and proof*

## Sections A, B and C

1 Copy and complete the first five terms of each of these linear sequences.

   (a) 4, 10, ____ , 22 , ____

   (b) 42, ____ , 34 , ____ , 26

   (c) $p, p + 3,$ ____ , ____ , ____

   (d) $s - 4,$ ___ , $s + 6 , s + 11,$ ___

2 These are the first four terms of a linear sequence.
   5, 9, 13, 17

   (a) What are the next two terms of the sequence?

   (b) Find an expression for the $n$th term of the sequence.

   (c) What is the 20th term of the sequence?

   (d) Show that 120 cannot be a term in this sequence.

   (e) Which term in this sequence is 105?

3 Match the expressions for the $n$th term to the correct sequence.

   A   $n^2 + n - 3$      B   $n^2 + n - 1$      C   $3n^2 + 2n - 6$
   D   $2n^2 + 3n - 4$     E   $2n^2 - 3n$        F   $4n - 3$

   (a) 1, 5, 9, 13            (b) 1, 5, 11, 19       (c) ⁻1, 10, 27, 50

   (d) ⁻1, 3, 9, 17         (e) ⁻1, 2, 9, 20       (f) 1, 10, 23, 40

4 A quadratic sequence begins 5, 9, 15, 23, …

   (a) Find the next two terms of this sequence.

   (b) Find an expression for the $n$th term of this sequence.

   (c) Show that 423 is the 20th term in this sequence.

5 Write down the first three terms of the sequence whose $n$th term is

   (a) $4n + 3$             (b) $n^4 + 2$          (c) $2n + 4$

   (d) $\dfrac{24}{n}$               (e) $\dfrac{n}{n + 3}$        (f) $n^3 - n^2$

6 Give the $n$th term of the following sequences.

   (a) 0, 3, 8, 15, 24, …

   (b) 2, 6, 12, 20, 30, …

   (c) 2, 6, 10, 14, 18 …

   (d) 1, 8, 27, 64, 125 …

   (e) $\dfrac{2}{3}, \dfrac{3}{7}, \dfrac{4}{11}, \dfrac{5}{15},$ …

   (f) 20, 17, 14, 11, 8 …

   (g) 2, 7, 14, 23, 34 …

## Section D

1 Show that each of these statements is false.

   A   $24x > 24$ for all values of $x$.

   B   $\frac{1}{2}x < x$ for all values of $x$.

   C   The difference between any two consecutive square numbers is prime.

2 In each of these statements $n$ is a positive integer.
State which one of the statements is false, and give a counter-example.

   A   $n^2 + 3n > {}^-2$ for all values of $n$

   B   $n^2 + 4n + 6$ is even for all values of $n$

   C   $n^2 - 2n > 15$ for all values of $n$ greater than 5

## Sections E and F

1 Points are marked on a circle, and chords are drawn joining all the points.

      1 point         2 points       3 points
      0 chords       1 chords      3 chords

  (a)  Find an expression for the number of chords if there are $n$ points on the circle.

  (b)  How many chords can be drawn if there are 20 points on the circle?

  (c)  If 66 chords can be drawn, how many points are there on the circle?

2 (a)  This diagram shows a square made with matches.
Explain from the diagram why the total number of matches is $2n(n + 1)$.

  (b)  Find a formula for the total number of matches in this diagram.

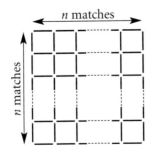

*n* matches

*n* matches

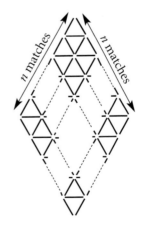

*n* matches    *n* matches

**3** Prove that the product of two positive numbers is always less than the square of the sum of them.

**4** Prove that the sum of the squares of two consecutive numbers is always odd.

**5** (a) Write expressions for four consecutive numbers, where the smallest is $p$.

(b) Prove that the sum of the four consecutive numbers is equal to the difference between the product of the last pair and the product of the first pair.

**6** (a) You can place a 3 by 3 square anywhere on this grid.

| 1 | 2 | 3 | 4 | 5 | 6 | 7 | 8 |
|---|---|---|---|---|---|---|---|
| 9 | 10 | 11 | 12 | 13 | 14 | 15 | 16 |
| 17 | 18 | 19 | 20 | 21 | 22 | 23 | 24 |
| 25 | 26 | 27 | 28 | 29 | 30 | 31 | 32 |
| 33 | 34 | 35 | 36 | 37 | 38 | 39 | 40 |
| 41 | 42 | 43 | 44 | 45 | 46 | 47 | 48 |
| 49 | 50 | 51 | 52 | 53 | 54 | 55 | 56 |
| 57 | 58 | 59 | 60 | 61 | 62 | 63 | 64 |
| 65 | 66 | 67 | 68 | 69 | 70 | 71 | 72 |

(i) If the lowest number in the square is $k$, write an expression for each of the corner numbers in the square.

(ii) Prove that the difference between the products of the opposite corners of the square is always 32.

*(b) Prove that the difference between the opposite corner products for any size square placed on this grid will be a multiple of 8.

*7 All prime numbers greater than 3 can be written in the form $6n + 1$ or $6n - 1$. Prove that the difference of the squares of any two prime numbers greater than 3 is a multiple of 12.

# 37 Histograms

## Section A

1 This histogram shows the distribution of the lengths of a group of babies.

Copy and complete this frequency table.

| Length, $l$ cm | Frequency |
|---|---|
| $60 < l \le 64$ | |
| $64 < l \le 66$ | |
| $66 < l \le 68$ | |
| $68 < l \le 70$ | |
| $70 < l \le 74$ | |

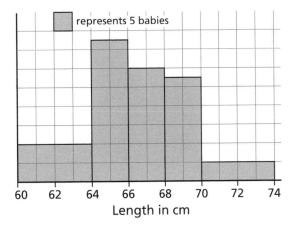

represents 5 babies

Length in cm

2 A company surveyed its employees to find out the distance they each travelled to work.

The results are summarised in the table below.

| Distance, $d$ km | Frequency |
|---|---|
| $0 < d \le 5$ | 10 |
| $5 < d \le 10$ | 22 |
| $10 < d \le 20$ | 15 |
| $20 < d \le 50$ | 6 |
| $50 < d$ | 0 |

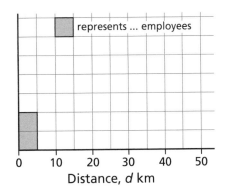

represents ... employees

Distance, $d$ km

The bar for $0 < d \le 5$ has been drawn.

(a) What does one square on the histogram represent?

(b) Copy and complete the histogram.

## Sections B and C

1 A survey was carried out to find out the amount of pocket money received each week by a group of secondary school pupils.

The distribution is shown in this histogram.

(a) How many pupils received less than £4 each week?

(b) How many pupils received more than £8 each week?

(c) How many pupils were surveyed altogether?

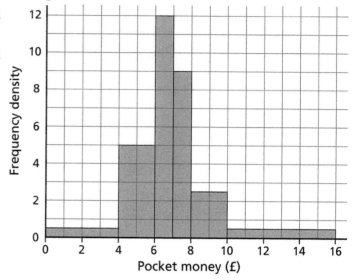

2 Copy and complete the frequency table below, using the information in the histogram.

| Weight, w g | Frequency |
|---|---|
| 20 < w ≤ 40 | |
| 40 < w ≤ 50 | |
| 50 < w ≤ 60 | |
| 60 < w ≤ 80 | |

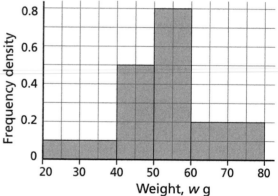

3 This table shows the distribution of the weights of a group of 15-year-old boys.

| Weight, w kg | Frequency |
|---|---|
| 30 < w ≤ 40 | 2 |
| 40 < w ≤ 50 | 10 |
| 50 < w ≤ 55 | 15 |
| 55 < w ≤ 60 | 13 |
| 60 < w ≤ 70 | 6 |
| 70 < w ≤ 90 | 4 |

(a) Calculate the frequency density for each interval.

(b) Draw a histogram for the data.

4 The unfinished histogram and table give information about the length of time taken by some members of a health club to run one mile.

Use the information to copy and complete the table and histogram.

| Time, t minutes | Frequency |
|---|---|
| 5 < t ≤ 8 | |
| 8 < t ≤ 9 | |
| 9 < t ≤ 10 | 13 |
| 10 < t ≤ 12 | 8 |
| 12 < t ≤ 14 | 2 |

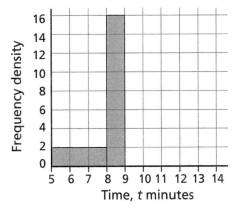

5 This table shows the distribution of ages of cars parked in a car park.

Draw a histogram for the data.

| Age, A years | Frequency |
|---|---|
| 0 < A ≤ 1 | 6 |
| 1 < A ≤ 3 | 27 |
| 3 < A ≤ 6 | 15 |
| 6 < A ≤ 10 | 14 |
| 10 < A ≤ 20 | 3 |

# 38 *Algebraic fractions and equations*

## Section A

**1** Find the value of the following when $x = {}^-1$, $y = \frac{1}{4}$ and $z = 4$.

    (a) $x^2y$               (b) $\frac{z}{x}$              (c) $\frac{z}{y}$              (d) $\frac{x^3}{y^2}$

**2** Simplify the following.

    (a) $m^3 \times m^4$        (b) $m^4 \div m^3$        (c) $(m^4)^3$           (d) $(m^3)^4$

**3** Simplify the following.

    (a) $\frac{4x^2y}{2y}$           (b) $\frac{x^2y^3}{xy^2}$          (c) $\frac{6a^3b^2}{2a^4b^5}$        (d) $\frac{3a^5b^3c^2}{12a^4b^4c^4}$

**4** Simplify the following.

    (a) $4x^3 \times 2x^2y^3$           (b) $x^{-3}y^2 \times xy^{-3}$        (c) $(2x^3y)^3$

    (d) $(x^4y^2)^3 \div x^5y^4$        (e) $\sqrt{\dfrac{16x^4y^2}{9p^6q^8}}$

**5** Write the following as simply as possible.

    (a) $\dfrac{6a + 9b}{3}$             (b) $\dfrac{3a + 21}{7}$             (c) $\dfrac{6ab - 12b^2}{3b}$

**6** Write each of the following as simply as possible as a single fraction.

    (a) $\dfrac{b + 3}{3} - \dfrac{b}{12}$               (b) $\frac{1}{3}(x + 4) + \frac{1}{12}(x - 3)$

    (c) $\dfrac{2a + 3b}{3a} - \dfrac{3a - b}{6a}$         (d) $\dfrac{3ab}{4} \times \dfrac{2a}{b}$

    (e) $\dfrac{4c}{d} \times \dfrac{cd}{2}$                (f) $\dfrac{3p}{2} \div \dfrac{2p}{3}$

    (g) $\dfrac{4a^2bc}{3} \div \dfrac{2ab^2c}{5}$

## Sections B and C

1 Simplify and express each of these each of these as a fraction in its simplest form.

   (a) $\dfrac{4a+6}{10a+15}$
        (b) $\dfrac{x-7}{x^2-5x-14}$
        (c) $\dfrac{x-3}{9-3x}$

2 By substituting a value for $x$ show that the following are **incorrect**, and explain what has been done incorrectly.

   (a) $\dfrac{\cancel{2}1}{x+\cancel{2}1}=\dfrac{1}{x+1}$
        (b) $\dfrac{\cancel{x}}{\cancel{x}+5}=\dfrac{1}{x+5}$

3 Simplify each of these by factorising and then cancelling.

   (a) $\dfrac{x^2+x-12}{x-3}$
        (b) $\dfrac{5x-25}{x^2-3x-10}$
        (c) $\dfrac{x^2-16}{x^2+2x-24}$

4 Copy and complete this simplification.

$$\dfrac{p^2-\blacksquare p-\blacksquare}{p^2-\blacksquare}=\dfrac{p-4}{p-3}$$

5 Write each of these as a single fraction. Simplify your answer where possible.

   (a) $\dfrac{3}{4a}+\dfrac{6}{a}$
        (b) $\dfrac{3}{x}+\dfrac{x}{5}$
        (c) $4-p^{-2}$

6 Write each of these as a single fraction.

   (a) $\dfrac{3}{x^2-9}+\dfrac{x}{x+3}$
     (b) $2+\dfrac{1}{x^2-1}+\dfrac{x}{x+1}$
     (c) $\dfrac{1}{3x+2}-\dfrac{1}{3x-5}$

## Sections D and E

1 Solve each of these.

   (a) $\dfrac{8}{x}+\dfrac{3x}{x+2}=4$
     (b) $\dfrac{3x}{x+1}+\dfrac{x}{x-1}=4$
     (c) $\dfrac{x-1}{x+1}=\dfrac{x+2}{x+6}$

2 Solve each of these (you should obtain a quadratic equation to solve).

   (a) $\dfrac{3}{x}+4x=13$
          (b) $\dfrac{5}{2x+1}+\dfrac{6}{x+1}=3$

   (c) $\dfrac{1}{x-1}-\dfrac{1}{x}=8$
        (d) $\dfrac{2}{y+1}+\dfrac{3}{2y+3}=1$

3 The sum of the reciprocals of two consecutive numbers is $\frac{7}{12}$. Find the numbers.

4 Rearrange each of the following to make the letter in the brackets the subject.

   (a) $R=\dfrac{st}{m}+\dfrac{sr}{m}$   $(t)$
        (b) $p=\dfrac{4(q+r)}{q-r}$   $(q)$

   (c) $\dfrac{a}{b}+\dfrac{c}{d}=e$   $(b)$
         (d) $S=\dfrac{y^2}{t}-\dfrac{x^2}{u}$   $(u)$

## Section F

1 (a) Simplify the expression $\frac{p}{4} + \frac{5p}{12} - \frac{p}{6}$.

(b) Solve the equation $\frac{1}{x-3} - \frac{3}{x+2} = \frac{1}{2}$.

2 Make $p$ the subject of the formula $r = \sqrt{\dfrac{7}{p-4}}$.

3 Find two consecutive integers whose reciprocals add up to $\frac{9}{20}$.

4 Factorise $x^2 + 2x - 255$.

5 Write $\dfrac{5}{x(x+1)} - \dfrac{2}{x^2}$ as a single fraction.

6 Karl was asked to write $\dfrac{6}{x-2} - \dfrac{4}{x+2}$ as a single fraction in its lowest terms.

Here is his solution.
Find the two mistakes that he made and write out the correct solution.

$$\frac{6}{x-2} - \frac{4}{x+2} = \frac{6(x+2) - 4(x-2)}{(x-2)(x+2)}$$

$$= \frac{6x + 12 - 4x - 8}{(x-2)(x+2)}$$

$$= \frac{2x + 4}{(x-2)(x+2)}$$

$$= \frac{2(\cancel{x+2})}{(x-2)(\cancel{x+2})} = \frac{2}{x-\cancel{2}} = \frac{1}{x-1}$$

✗ see me Karl

7 Pam is training for a long-distance cycle race.
One day she cycles for $x$ hours and travels a distance of 112 km.

(a) Write down, in terms of $x$, Pam's average speed in km/h.

The next day she cycles for one hour more to travel the same distance and her average speed is 2 km/h slower than the day before.

(b) Show that $x^2 + x - 56 = 0$.

(c) Calculate the number of hours Pam cycles on the second day.

# Mixed questions 9

1  Find all the possible values of $x$ between $0°$ and $360°$ for each of these.

(a)  $\sin 2x = 0.5$     (b)  $\cos\left(\frac{x}{2}\right) = {}^-0.2$    (c)  $\tan 3x = 2$       (d)  $5 \cos 2x = {}^-3$

2  Write down the first five terms of the sequences that have the following $n$th terms.

(a)  $4n - 3$         (b)  $2 - 3n^2$          (c)  $n^3 + 2n^2 - 1$      (d)  $\frac{3}{n}$

3  Hayley trains regularly at a health club.
   She runs on the treadmill for $4$ km at $x$ km/h then she cycles for $3$ km at $(x - 5)$ km/h.

(a)  Hayley exercises for exactly 1 hour.
     Form an equation in $x$ and show that it simplifies to  $x^2 - 12x + 20 = 0$.

(b)  Solve this equation and find the speeds at which Hayley runs and cycles.

4  A group of students were surveyed to find out the
   number of text messages they sent in a week.

   The distribution is shown in this histogram.

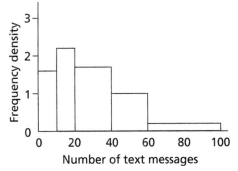

(a)  How many students sent
     fewer than 10 text messages?

(b)  How many students sent
     more than 40 text messages?

(c)  How many students were
     surveyed altogether?

(d)  Estimate the number of students
     who sent between 30 and 40 texts in a week.

5  Solve these inequalities.

(a)  $x + 5 \geq \frac{x+2}{4}$         (b)  $\frac{x-3}{2} \leq \frac{x}{5}$          (c)  $1 \leq 2x + 4 < 7$

6  This is a sketch of the graph  $y = \cos x$.
   Sketch the following graphs.

(a)  $y = 3 \cos x$

(b)  $y = {}^-\cos (3x)$

(c)  $y = \cos x + 3$

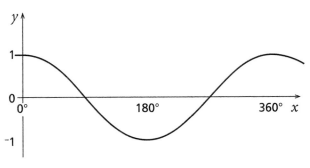

**7** Prove that the sum of any six consecutive numbers is a multiple of 3.

**8** (a) The graph of the equation $x^2 + y^2 = a^2$ is a circle.
Rearrange this equation to make $y$ the subject.

(b) The graph of the equation $\dfrac{x^2}{a^2} - \dfrac{y^2}{b^2} = 1$ is a curve called a hyperbola.
Rearrange this equation to make $y$ the subject.

**9** One light-year is about $9.4 \times 10^{12}$ km.
Alpha Centauri is the closest star to Earth. It is 4.34 light-years from Earth.

How many kilometres is it from Alpha Centauri to Earth?

**10** A line has equation $y = 4x - 3$.

(a) What is the gradient of the line?

(b) What are the coordinates of the $y$-intercept?

(c) Find the equation of the line perpendicular to the line $y = 4x - 3$, which passes through the point $(0, 4)$.

**11** The price of a washing machine is reduced by 15% in a sale.
The reduced price is £331.50.

(a) Calculate the original price of the washing machine.

(b) The shop offers 6 months interest-free credit on all sale goods.
They ask for a deposit of 20% of the sale price and then six equal payments of the remainder.

Calculate the deposit and monthly payments for the washing machine.

**12** Solve these pairs of simultaneous equations.

(a) $4x + y = 18$
    $3x + 2y = 7$

(b) $y = x^2 - 2$
    $y = 2x + 1$

**13** A, B, C and D are points on the circumference of a circle.
O is the centre of the circle.

Calculate these angles, giving reasons for each step of your working.

(a) Angle ABC

(b) Angle BCO

(c) Angle ADC

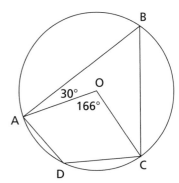

**14** Make $T_1$ the subject of the formula $W = \dfrac{R}{1-n}(T_2 - T_1)$.

**15** This vase is a frustum of a cone.
Calculate its volume.

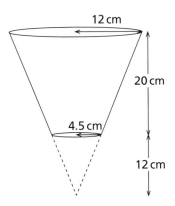

12 cm

20 cm

4.5 cm

12 cm

**16** This table shows the distribution of weights of
a group of babies at their 6-month health check.

(a) Make a cumulative frequency table.

(b) Draw a cumulative frequency graph
of the distribution.

(c) Estimate

    (i)   the median weight

    (ii)  the lower quartile

    (iii) the upper quartile

    (iv) the interquartile range

| Weight ($w$ kg) | Frequency |
|---|---|
| $6.0 < w \le 6.5$ | 8 |
| $6.5 < w \le 7.0$ | 10 |
| $7.0 < w \le 7.5$ | 24 |
| $7.5 < w \le 8.0$ | 35 |
| $8.0 < w \le 8.5$ | 33 |
| $8.5 < w \le 9.0$ | 21 |
| $9.0 < w \le 9.5$ | 15 |
| $9.5 < w \le 10.0$ | 4 |

**17** Write each of these as a single fraction.

(a) $\dfrac{r+1}{2} + \dfrac{2r-1}{3r}$      (b) $\dfrac{b}{3} - \dfrac{4-3b}{2}$      (c) $\dfrac{4e^2}{5} \times \dfrac{3}{2e}$      (d) $\dfrac{4s^2t}{3} \div \dfrac{6s^2t}{t}$

**18** (a) Work out how many matchsticks would be needed
for each of the first five of these patterns.

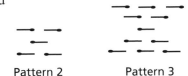

Pattern 1          Pattern 2          Pattern 3

(b) Find a rule for the number of matchsticks in the $n$th pattern.

(c) One of these matchstick patterns can be made using 419 matchsticks.
Which pattern is it?

# 39 Indices 2

## Section A

**1** Write each of these as a single power of 3.

(a) $3^3 \times 3^5$    (b) $3 \times 3^4$    (c) $\dfrac{3^9}{3^3}$    (d) $(3^5)^4$    (e) $\dfrac{1}{3^6}$

(f) $3 \times 3^7 \times 3^8$    (g) $\dfrac{3^5 \times 3^4}{3^2}$    (h) $\dfrac{3^7}{3^1}$    (i) $(3^{-3})^4$    (j) $(3^{-6})^{-2}$

**2** (a) Copy and complete this list of the first six powers of 3: $3^1 = 3$, $3^2 = 9$, $3^3 = 27$, ...

(b) Write each of these as a power of 3.

(i) $243 \times 27$    (ii) $\dfrac{81}{729}$    (iii) $\dfrac{1}{27 \times 81}$    (iv) $243^2$    (v) $729^5$

**3** Find the value of $n$ in each of these equations.

(a) $3^n = 243 \times 81$    (b) $3^n = \dfrac{729}{9}$    (c) $3^n = \sqrt{729}$    (d) $3^n = \dfrac{1}{243}$

(e) $3^{n+1} = 243$    (f) $3^{n-1} = 729$    (g) $3^{2n} = \dfrac{1}{81^2}$    (h) $3^{3n} = 729^2$

**4** (a) Copy and complete this list of the first six powers of 5: $5^1 = 5$, $5^2 = 25$, $5^3 = 125$, ...

(b) Write each of these as a power of 5.

(i) $\sqrt{15625}$    (ii) $\dfrac{25}{3125}$    (iii) $\dfrac{1}{625^2}$    (iv) $3125^8$    (v) $625^{-5}$

## Sections B and C

**1** Find the value of each of these.

(a) $625^{\frac{1}{2}}$    (b) $(\frac{1}{9})^{\frac{1}{2}}$    (c) $(\frac{1}{16})^{-\frac{1}{2}}$    (d) $100^{\frac{1}{2}} \times 36^{\frac{1}{2}}$    (e) $(0.04)^{\frac{1}{2}}$

**2** Find the value of each of these.

(a) $8^{\frac{1}{3}}$    (b) $125^{-\frac{1}{3}}$    (c) $1000^{-\frac{1}{3}}$    (d) $(\frac{1}{8})^{-\frac{1}{3}}$    (e) $(0.008)^{\frac{1}{3}}$

**3** Find the value of each of these.

(a) $27^{\frac{2}{3}}$    (b) $16^{\frac{3}{2}}$    (c) $81^{\frac{3}{4}}$    (d) $64^{\frac{2}{3}}$    (e) $625^{\frac{3}{2}}$

**4** Find the value of each of these.

(a) $125^{-\frac{2}{3}}$    (b) $9^{\frac{3}{2}}$    (c) $16^{-\frac{3}{2}}$    (d) $1000^{\frac{2}{3}}$    (e) $(\frac{1}{9})^{-1.5}$

## Sections D, E and F

1  Use a calculator to find the following, to four significant figures.

   (a)  $1.3^7$       (b)  $5^{0.5}$       (c)  $\sqrt[4]{8}$       (d)  $6.5^{1.8}$       (e)  $0.9^{\frac{2}{3}}$

2  This graph shows the population of a colony of animals.
   When measurements started, the population was 100.
   The population, $P$, after $t$ years is given by the equation

$$P = 100 \times 1.3^t$$

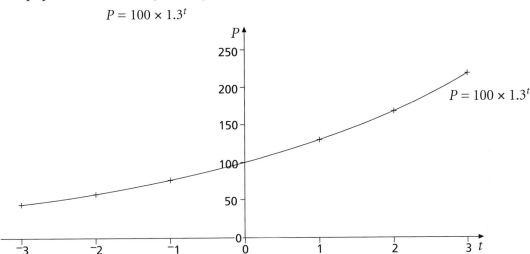

   (a)  By what percentage does the population increase in each year?

   (b)  Calculate, to two significant figures, the value of $P$ when $t = 2.5$.
        Check from the graph.

   (c)  Do the same for the value of $P$ when $t = {}^-1.5$.

   (d)  Use trial and improvement to find, to two decimal places, the value of $t$
        for which $P = 200$.

3  The population of a region appears to fit the formula

$$P = 5000 \times 2^{0.01n}$$

   where $P$ is the population $n$ years after the year 2000.

   (a)  What was the population in the year 2000?

   (b)  Show that the population has doubled by the year 2100.

   (c)  By which year will the population be 8 times what it was in the year 2000?

4  An object is heated and then allowed to cool.
   Its temperature $T°C$ after cooling for $t$ minutes is given by the formula  $T = 45 \times 1.2^{-t}$.

   (a)  Calculate, to the nearest °C, its temperature after cooling for 8 minutes.

   (b)  Draw a rough sketch to show the shape of the graph of $T$ against $t$.

# 40 *Vectors*

## Sections A, B and C

1  Vectors $\mathbf{a} = \begin{bmatrix} 2 \\ 3 \end{bmatrix}$ and $\mathbf{b} = \begin{bmatrix} 1 \\ -2 \end{bmatrix}$.

For each of the following write down the column vector.
Draw a diagram representing the vector.

(a)  $\mathbf{a} + \mathbf{b}$        (b)  $2\mathbf{a} + \mathbf{b}$        (c)  $3\mathbf{a} + 2\mathbf{b}$        (d)  $\mathbf{a} - \mathbf{b}$

2  PQRS is a parallelogram. $\overrightarrow{PQ} = \mathbf{x}$ and $\overrightarrow{PS} = \mathbf{y}$.
Express each of these vectors in terms of $\mathbf{x}$ and $\mathbf{y}$.

(a)  $\overrightarrow{RQ}$        (b)  $\overrightarrow{PR}$

(c)  $\overrightarrow{QS}$        (d)  $\overrightarrow{SQ}$

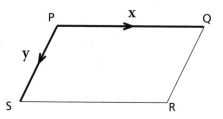

3  On this grid $\overrightarrow{OA} = \mathbf{a}$ and $\overrightarrow{OB} = \mathbf{b}$.
Write these vectors using $\mathbf{a}$ and $\mathbf{b}$.

(a)  $\overrightarrow{OF}$        (b)  $\overrightarrow{DM}$        (c)  $\overrightarrow{OD}$

(d)  $\overrightarrow{AL}$        (e)  $\overrightarrow{BA}$        (f)  $\overrightarrow{JF}$

(g)  $\overrightarrow{AI}$        (h)  $\overrightarrow{LB}$

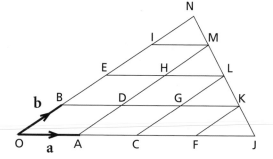

4  ABCDEFGH is a regular octagon.

$\overrightarrow{OA} = \mathbf{u}$        $\overrightarrow{OB} = \mathbf{v}$        $\overrightarrow{OC} = \mathbf{w}$

(a)  Express these in terms of $\mathbf{u}$, $\mathbf{v}$ and $\mathbf{w}$.

(i)  $\overrightarrow{GC}$        (ii)  $\overrightarrow{OF}$        (iii)  $\overrightarrow{AB}$        (iv)  $\overrightarrow{AC}$

(b)  Express these in terms of $\mathbf{v}$ and $\mathbf{w}$.

(i)  $\overrightarrow{BC}$        (ii)  $\overrightarrow{GB}$        (iii)  $\overrightarrow{GF}$        (iv)  $\overrightarrow{FC}$

(c)  What do your results in (b) tell you about
quadrilateral BCFG?

5  A, B, C and D are the vertices of a quadrilateral.
$\overrightarrow{AB} = 2\overrightarrow{DC}$

(a)  What can you say about sides AB and DC?

(b)  What can you say about the quadrilateral?

## Sections D and E

**1** On this grid $\overrightarrow{OX} = \mathbf{x}$ and $\overrightarrow{OY} = \mathbf{y}$.

Express in terms of $\mathbf{x}$ and $\mathbf{y}$ the position vectors of P, Q, R, S and T.

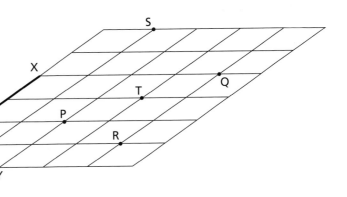

**2** Write these expressions as vectors in their simplest form.

(a) $\mathbf{x} + \mathbf{y} + \mathbf{x} + 2\mathbf{y}$

(b) $2\mathbf{x} + \mathbf{y} - \frac{1}{2}\mathbf{y}$

(c) $\mathbf{x} - \frac{1}{2}(\mathbf{x} + \mathbf{y})$

(d) $\mathbf{y} - \frac{1}{2}(\mathbf{x} - \mathbf{y})$

(e) $3(\mathbf{x} - 2\mathbf{y})$

(f) $\frac{1}{3}\mathbf{x} + \frac{2}{3}\mathbf{y} - \frac{1}{2}\mathbf{x} - \frac{1}{2}\mathbf{y}$

**3** ABCD is a kite.

$\overrightarrow{AC} = \mathbf{p}$ and $\overrightarrow{BD} = \mathbf{q}$.

X is the point where the diagonals AC and BD intersect. X divides AC in the ratio $2:1$.

Write down expressions for

(a) $\overrightarrow{AD}$     (b) $\overrightarrow{AB}$

(c) $\overrightarrow{DC}$     (d) $\overrightarrow{CB}$

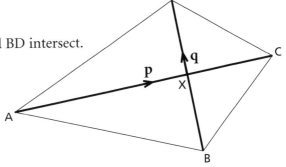

**4** OAB is a triangle with $\overrightarrow{OA} = \mathbf{a}$ and $\overrightarrow{OB} = \mathbf{b}$.

M is the midpoint of AB.

(a) Write down an expression for $\overrightarrow{AB}$.

(b) Find, and simplify, an expression for $\overrightarrow{OM}$.

**5** In this diagram $\overrightarrow{OP} = \mathbf{u} + 2\mathbf{v}$ and $\overrightarrow{PQ} = \mathbf{v} - \mathbf{u}$.

(a) Find $\overrightarrow{OQ}$ in terms of $\mathbf{u}$ and $\mathbf{v}$.

(b) Hence find $\mathbf{v}$ in the form $\begin{bmatrix} m \\ n \end{bmatrix}$.

(c) Write $\mathbf{u}$ in the form $\begin{bmatrix} m \\ n \end{bmatrix}$.

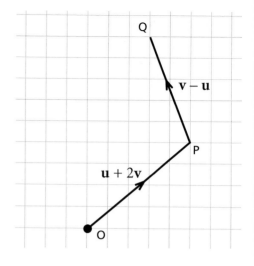

## Section F

**1** In parallelogram ABCD, let $\overrightarrow{AB} = \mathbf{x}$ and $\overrightarrow{AD} = \mathbf{y}$.
Let the midpoint of diagonal AC be M.
Let the midpoint of diagonal BD be N.

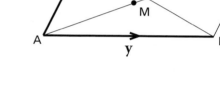

(a) Express these in terms of $\mathbf{x}$ and $\mathbf{y}$.

(i) $\overrightarrow{AC}$　　(ii) $\overrightarrow{AM}$

(b) Express these in terms of $\mathbf{x}$ and $\mathbf{y}$.

(i) $\overrightarrow{BD}$　　(ii) $\overrightarrow{BN}$　　(iii) $\overrightarrow{AN}$

(c) Explain why your answers show that the diagonals of a parallelogram bisect each other.

**2** A, B and C are three points with position vectors
$\overrightarrow{OA} = \mathbf{u}$, $\overrightarrow{OB} = \mathbf{v}$ and $\overrightarrow{OC} = 2\mathbf{v} - \mathbf{u}$.

(a) Find vectors $\overrightarrow{AB}$ and $\overrightarrow{BC}$ in terms of $\mathbf{u}$ and $\mathbf{v}$.

(b) Explain why your answers to (a) show that
A, B and C lie in a straight line.

**3** ABCD is a parallelogram.

$\overrightarrow{AB} = \mathbf{p}$　　　　$\overrightarrow{AD} = \mathbf{q}$

R, S, T and U are points on the sides AB, BC,
CD and DA such that in each case the point
divides the line in the ratio $1:3$.

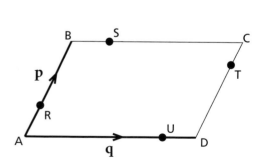

(a) Express $\overrightarrow{RS}$ in terms of $\mathbf{p}$ and $\mathbf{q}$.

(b) Express $\overrightarrow{UT}$ in terms of $\mathbf{p}$ and $\mathbf{q}$.

(c) What type of quadrilateral is RSTU?
Justify your answer.

**4** In the diagram $\overrightarrow{OA} = \mathbf{a}$ and $\overrightarrow{OB} = \mathbf{b}$.

A is the midpoint of OX.
B divides OY in the ratio $1:2$.

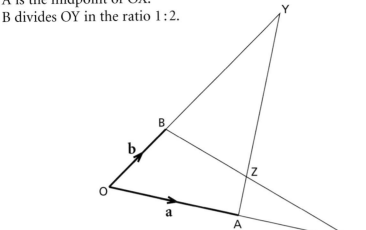

(a) Write expressions, in terms of **a** and **b**, for

    (i) $\overrightarrow{OY}$     (ii) $\overrightarrow{AY}$      (iii) $\overrightarrow{OX}$      (iv) $\overrightarrow{BX}$

(b) $\overrightarrow{AZ} = h\overrightarrow{AY}$ where $h$ is a fraction.
Write and simplify an expression for $\overrightarrow{OZ}$ in terms of **a**, **b** and $h$.

(c) Similarly, $\overrightarrow{BZ} = k\overrightarrow{BX}$.
Write an expression for $\overrightarrow{OZ}$ in terms of **a**, **b** and $k$.

(d) Since the two expressions for $\overrightarrow{OZ}$ found in (b) and (c) must be equal,
form a pair of simultaneous equations in $h$ and $k$.
Use these to find the value of $h$.

(e) Hence write down the ratio in which Z divides AY.

# 41 Transforming graphs

## Sections A and B

1 Find the minimum value of each expression and the value of $x$ that gives this minimum.
   (a) $(x-5)^2 + 1$     (b) $(x+3)^2 + 2$     (c) $(x-1)^2 - 4$     (d) $(x+8)^2$

2 Three of these equations match the graphs.

$y = (x+2)^2 + 4$

$y = (x-2)^2 + 4$

$y = (x+4)^2 + 2$

$y = (x-4)^2 + 2$

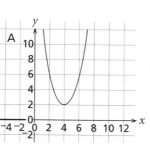

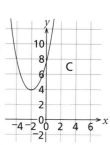

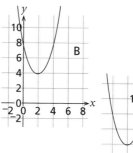

   (a) Match each graph with its appropriate equation.
   (b) Sketch the missing graph.

3 For each of the following three functions …

P $\boxed{y = (x-2)^2 - 9}$     Q $\boxed{y = (x+1)^2 - 4}$     R $\boxed{y = (x-5)^2 - 25}$

   (a) Find the minimum point on the graph.
   (b) Work out where the graph will cut the $x$-axis.
   (c) Work out where the graph will cut the $y$-axis.
   (d) Sketch the graph marking all the points you have found.

4 Complete the square for each expression.
   (a) $x^2 + 8x + 10$          (b) $x^2 - 6x + 12$          (c) $x^2 + 2x - 3$

5 The expression $x^2 - 10x + 28$ can be written in the form $(x-a)^2 + b$.
   (a) Find the values of $a$ and $b$.
   (b) Hence find the minimum point on the graph of $y = x^2 - 10x + 28$.
   (c) Sketch this graph, showing the minimum point and the $y$-intercept.

6 The expression $x^2 - 20x$ can be written in the form $(x-p)^2 - q$.
   Find the values of $p$ and $q$ and hence the minimum value of the expression.

7 (a) Expand $(2x+5)^2$.
   (b) Write $4x^2 + 20x + 23$ in the form $(ax+b)^2 + c$.
   (c) State the minimum value of the expression $4x^2 + 20x + 23$ and the value of $x$
       for which it occurs.

## Sections C and D

1 Each of these diagrams show two curves.
All four curves (A, B, C and D) are transformations of $y = x^2$.

Find the equation of each curve.

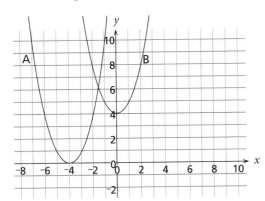 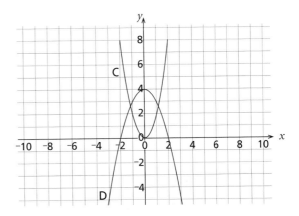

2 Find the equations of the images of each these graphs after a stretch of scale
factor $\frac{1}{2}$ in the $y$-direction followed by a translation of $\begin{bmatrix} 0 \\ -2 \end{bmatrix}$.

(a) $y = x^2$                (b) $y = x$

3 On the same axes sketch and label the graphs of $y = x^2 - 1$, $y = 2x^2 - 1$ and $y = \frac{1}{2}x^2 - 1$.

4 The graph of $y = \sin x$ is shown for $^-180° \le x \le 180°$.
On separate diagrams sketch each pair of graphs
for $^-180° \le x \le 180°$.

(a) $y = 2\sin x$ and $y = ^-2\sin x$,

(b) $y = \sin\frac{1}{2}x$ and $y = ^-\sin\frac{1}{2}x$

(c) $y = ^-\sin x$ and $y = 2 - \sin x$

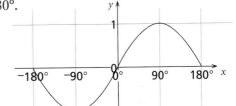

5 (a) Sketch the graph of $y = \sin(x - 90°)$.

(b) What transformation could you apply to the graph of $y = \sin(x - 90°)$
so that the image is $y = \cos x$?

**6** Each graph is the image of $y = \cos x$ after a transformation.
Write the equation of each graph.

(a)

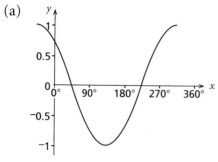

(b)

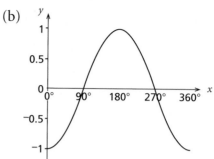

(c)

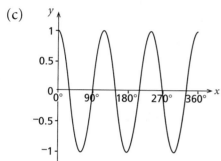

## Sections E and F

**1** (a) If $f(x) = 4x + 1$ and $g(x) = 2x - 5$, evaluate

    (i) $f(2)$       (ii) $g(3)$       (iii) $f(^-1)$       (iv) $g(^-1)$

 (b) If $f(x) = g(x)$ find the value of $x$.

**2** (a) If $f(x) = x^2 - 2$, evaluate

    (i) $f(3)$       (ii) $f(0)$       (iii) $f(^-2)$

 (b) If $f(x) = 34$ what are the possible values of $x$?

 (c) If $g(x) = 5x - 2$ for what values of $x$ is $f(x) = g(x)$?

**3** (a) If $f(x) = 3x - 1$, evaluate

    (i) $f(2)$       (ii) $f(0)$

 (b) If $y = f(x + 2)$, find the value of $y$ when

    (i) $x = 1$       (ii) $x = 0$

 (c) Which of these gives the rule for $y$ in terms of $x$?

| $y = 3x + 1$ | $y = 3x + 5$ | $y = x + 1$ | $y = 3x + 6$ |

**4** $f(x) = x^2$ and $y = f(2x)$.

 (a) Find the value of $y$ when     (i) $x = 1$       (ii) $x = 2$       (iii) $x = ^-5$

 (b) Write the rule for $y$ in terms of $x$.

**5** $f(x) = \cos x$ and $y = f(x - 90°)$

   (a) Write the rule for $y$ in terms of $x$.

   (b) Sketch the graph of $y = f(x - 90°)$ for $0° \le x \le 360°$.

**6** If $f(x) = x^2 - 3$, write each of the following rules for $y$ in terms of $x$.
Expand any brackets and write each rule in its simplest form.

   (a) $y = f(x) + 2$      (b) $y = f(x + 2)$      (c) $y = 2f(x)$      (d) $y = f(2x)$

**7** The diagram shows part of the graph
of $y = f(x)$.
On separate grids draw the graph of
each of the transformed functions below.

In each case label the transformed
point P′ with its coordinates.

   (a) $y = f(x + 2)$

   (b) $y = {}^-f(x)$

   (c) $y = \frac{1}{2}f(x)$

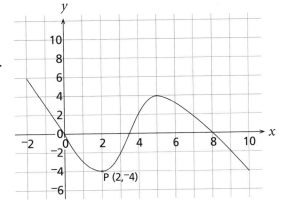

**8** The diagram shows part of the graph of $y = f(x)$.
The point marked A is the maximum point on the graph.

Write down the coordinates for the maximum point for
each of the following curves.

   (a) $y = f(x) - 1$

   (b) $y = f(x - 1)$

   (c) $y = 2f(x)$

   (d) $y = f(2x)$

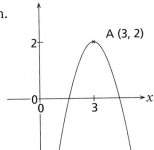

**9** The diagram shows part of the graph of $y = f(x)$.
On separate grids draw

   (a) $y = \frac{1}{2}f(x)$

   (b) $y = f(x) + 1$

   (c) $y = f(\frac{1}{2}x)$

   (d) $y = 2 - f(x)$

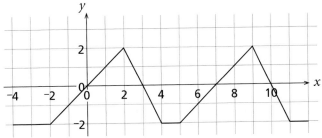

147

## Section G

**1** The table shows pairs of values of $v$ and $s$. It is thought that $v$ and $s$ are connected by a relationship of the form $s = av^2 + b$.

| $v$ | 1 | 1.5 | 2 | 2.5 |
|---|---|---|---|---|
| $s$ | 2 | 7 | 14 | 23 |

(a) Make a table of values of $v^2$ and $s$.

(b) Draw the graph of $s$ against $v^2$.

(c) Use your graph to find the values of $a$ and $b$.

(d) Write down the relationship connecting $v^2$ and $s$.

**2** In an experiment it is expected that values of $P$ and $h$ are connected by a formula of the form $P = \frac{a}{h} + b$.

| $h$ | 1.6 | 2.0 | 2.5 | 2.7 | 3.0 |
|---|---|---|---|---|---|
| $P$ | 3.4 | 3 | 2.7 | 2.6 | 2.5 |

(a) Tabulate values of $\frac{1}{h}$ and $P$, and graph $P$ against $\frac{1}{h}$.

(b) Use your graph to find the values of $a$ and $b$ and hence write down the relationship connecting $P$ and $h$.

(c) Use your relationship to work out the value of $P$ if $h = 1.8$.

**3** The table shows pairs of values found in an experiment. It is thought that $p$ and $q$ are connected by a relationship of the type $p = a\sqrt{q} + b$.

| $q$ | 14 | 22 | 26 | 31 |
|---|---|---|---|---|
| $p$ | 23 | 30 | 33 | 37 |

By drawing a suitable graph find the values of $a$ and $b$.

**4** It is expected that $x$ and $y$ are connected by the relationship $y = \frac{a}{x^2} + b$.

| $x$ | 2 | 5 | 7 | 10 |
|---|---|---|---|---|
| $y$ | 12 | 3.6 | 2.8 | 2.4 |

(a) By drawing a suitable graph find the values of $a$ and $b$.

(b) Use your relationship between $y$ and $x$ to calculate the likely value of $y$ when $x = 4$.

# Mixed questions 10

1 (a) Find, as a fraction, the exact value of $\left(\frac{36}{25}\right)^{-\frac{1}{2}}$.

   (b) Find the value of $t$ if
   
   (i) $2^t = \frac{1}{8}$        (ii) $9^t = \frac{1}{3}$        (iii) $4^t = 8$

2 A hosepipe delivers water at the rate of 540 litres per hour.

   (a) How many litres does it deliver in 7 minutes?

   (b) How many seconds does it take to deliver one litre?

3 The function $f(x)$ is defined for values of $x$ in the interval $^-3 \leq x \leq 3$.
   The graph of $y = f(x)$ is shown in diagram A below.

   (a) Which of the diagrams shows each of these graphs?

   (i) $y = \frac{1}{2}f(x)$     (ii) $y = ^-2f(x)$     (iii) $y = ^-f(^-x)$     (iv) $y = f(x) - 2$

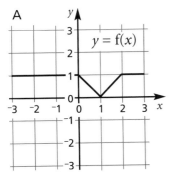
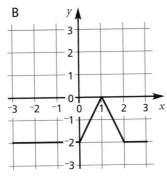
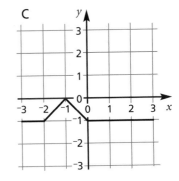
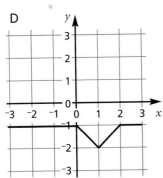
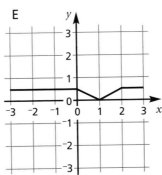
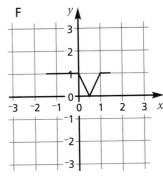

   (b) One of the diagrams has not been used yet. What graph does it show?

4 The surface areas of two similar capsules are $120\,\text{mm}^2$ and $270\,\text{mm}^2$.
   If the volume of the smaller capsule is $40\,\text{mm}^3$, what is the volume of the larger capsule?

5 If two integers differ by 2, prove that their squares differ by a multiple of 4.

**6** In this diagram, $\overrightarrow{OA} = \mathbf{a}$ and $\overrightarrow{OB} = \mathbf{b}$.

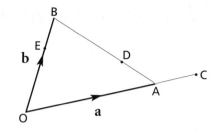

C is the point such that $\overrightarrow{AC} = \frac{1}{3}\mathbf{a}$.
D is one-third of the way along AB.
E is two-thirds of the way along OB.

(a) Express in terms of $\mathbf{a}$ and $\mathbf{b}$
   (i) $\overrightarrow{AB}$   (ii) $\overrightarrow{AD}$
(b) Prove that $\overrightarrow{CD} = \overrightarrow{DE}$.

**7** Two circles intersect at A and B.
AX and AY are diameters of the circles.

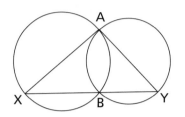

(a) Prove that XBY is a straight line.
(b) If AX = 10 cm, AY = 8 cm and XB = 7 cm,
   calculate the area of triangle AXY,
   correct to one decimal place.

**8** This triangle is right-angled at B.

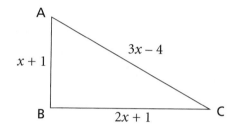

(a) Show that $x$ must satisfy the
   equation $2x^2 - 15x + 7 = 0$
(b) Solve the equation to find $x$.
(c) Write down the value of $\tan C$.

**9** Give a possible equation for each of these graphs.

(a)    (b)    (c)

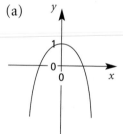
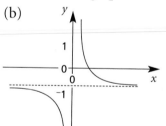
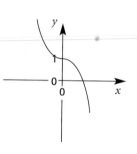

**\*10** A circle drawn inside a triangle so that all three sides of the triangle
are tangents to the circle is called the 'incircle' of the triangle.

(a) Find the radius of the incircle of right-angled triangle ABC.

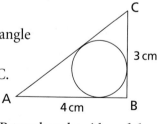

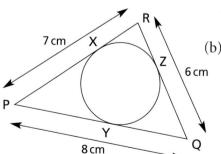

(b) The incircle of triangle PQR touches the sides of the
   triangle at points X, Y and Z, as shown in the diagram.
   Calculate lengths PX, QY and RZ.

# 42 *Congruent triangles*

## Sections A and B

1 These sketches are not drawn accurately.

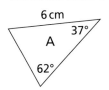 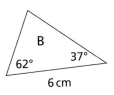  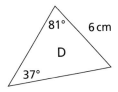

(a) Find two triangles that are congruent.

(b) Give the reason why they are congruent.

2 In this diagram, PM is perpendicular to the line *l*.
A is a point such that PA = PM.
The bisector of angle APM meets the line *l* at X.

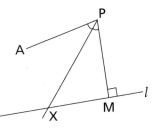

(a) Prove that triangles APX and MPX are congruent.

(b) What can you deduce about angle PAX?

## Sections C and D

1 ABC is an isosceles triangle, with AB = AC.
BM is perpendicular to AC.
CN is parallel to BA.
AN is perpendicular to CN.

By first proving that triangles ABM and CAN are
congruent, prove that BM = AN.

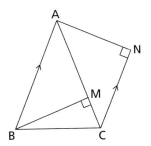

2 This is a construction for drawing at a point X
an angle equal to a given angle BAC.

- Draw an arc of a circle with centre A to cut
  AB at P and AC at Q.

- Draw an arc of the same radius with centre X.

- Set the compasses to a radius equal to PQ.
  Choose a point R on the arc with centre X.
  Draw the arc RS.
  Then angle RXS = angle BAC.

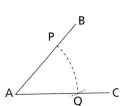

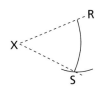

Use congruent triangles to prove
that this construction is correct.

# 43 Circles and equations

## Sections B and C

1 Sketch the circle with equation $x^2 + y^2 = 81$.

2 The diagram shows three concentric circles, centred at the origin, with their intercepts marked on the $x$-axis.

Write down the equation of each circle.

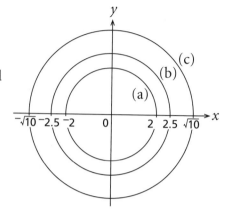

3 Write down the radius of each of these circles.
   (a) $x^2 + y^2 = 144$      (b) $x^2 + y^2 = 30$      (c) $x^2 + y^2 = 1$

4 Write down the equation of the circle with centre $(0, 0)$ and radius
   (a) 11      (b) $\sqrt{15}$      (c) $\frac{1}{5}$      (d) $2\sqrt{3}$

5 A circle has centre at the origin and passes through point $(0, 7)$. What is its equation?

6 A circle has centre at the origin and passes through the point $(6, 8)$.
   (a) What is the radius of the circle?
   (b) Write down the equation of the circle.

7 The diagram shows a sketch of the circle $x^2 + y^2 = 40$ and the line $y = x - 4$.
   (a) For the points of intersection A and B show that $x^2 - 4x - 12 = 0$.
   (b) Hence find the coordinates of the points of intersection of the line $y = x - 4$ and the circle $x^2 + y^2 = 40$.

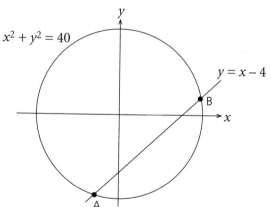

8 Find the coordinates of the two points where the line $x + y = 2$ crosses the circle $x^2 + y^2 = 52$.

**9** Find the points of intersection of the circle $x^2 + y^2 = 65$ and the line $y = 2x - 10$.

**10** Use graph paper for this question, using a scale of 2 cm to one unit, with both axes numbered from $^-5$ to 5.

(a) Draw the line $y = x - 2$.

(b) Draw the circle with centre at the origin and radius 4.

(c) Use the graph to write down the coordinates of the points where the line crosses the circle, as accurately as you can.

(d) Write down the equation of the circle.

(e) By solving a pair of simultaneous equations, write down the coordinates of the points of intersection of the line and the circle, correct to two decimal places.

**11** Find, correct to two decimal places, the coordinates of the points of intersection of the line $y = x + 2$ and the circle $x^2 + y^2 = 12$.

**12** Find, correct to two decimal places, the coordinates of the points of intersection of the line $y = 2x - 1$ and the circle $x^2 + y^2 = 7$.

**13** Match up the following three pairs of equations with the three statements below. Explain your method.

(a) $x^2 + y^2 = 14$
   $y = x - 4$

(b) $x^2 + y^2 = 6$
   $y = x + 4$

(c) $x^2 + y^2 = 18$
   $y = x + 6$

X   The equations represent a line and a circle that do not cross.

Y   The equations represent a circle and a line tangent to the circle.

Z   The equations represent a line and a circle that intersect at two points.

**14** Solve these pairs of simultaneous equations, giving your solutions correct to two decimal places when appropriate.

(a) $x^2 + y^2 = 45$
   $y - x = 3$

(b) $x^2 + y^2 = 19$
   $2x + y = 3$

(c) $y = x - 1$
   $2x^2 + y^2 = 15$

**15** Solve these pairs of simultaneous equations.

(a) $4x^2 + y^2 = 18$
   $2x - y = 0$

(b) $3x^2 + y^2 = 4$
   $y + 3x = 2$

(c) $y - x = 1$
   $4x^2 + y^2 = 4$

## Section D

1 Sketch the circle with equation $(x-4)^2 + (y-1)^2 = 9$.

2 Match up each circle with its equation.
Two of the equations are not needed.

P   $(x-4)^2 + (y+2)^2 = 4$
Q   $(x-4)^2 + (y-4)^2 = 16$
R   $(x+4)^2 + (y+4)^2 = 16$
S   $(x-4)^2 + (y-6)^2 = 4$
T   $(x+4)^2 + (y+6)^2 = 4$
U   $(x+2)^2 + (y-4)^2 = 4$

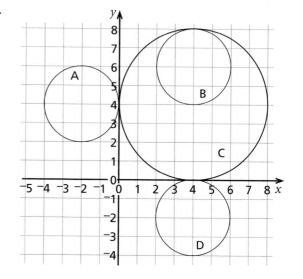

3 Write down the equation of the circle with radius 8 and centre $(2, 7)$.

4 Where does the circle $(x-5)^2 + (y-2)^2 = 40$ cut the $x$-axis?

5 Give the centre and radius of each of the following circles.
(a) $(x+3)^2 + (y-6)^2 = 100$
(b) $(x-8)^2 + (y+4)^2 = 1$
(c) $(x+2)^2 + (y+2.5)^2 = 4$
(d) $x^2 + (y-\frac{1}{2})^2 = 6\frac{1}{4}$

*6 Find the equations of these circles.
(a) Centre $(^-5, 3)$ and radius 9
(b) Centre $(^-4, 0)$ and passing through the origin
(c) Centre $(8, ^-6)$ and passing through the origin
(d) Centre $(0, ^-2)$ and passing through $(0, 6)$

*7 (a) Write $x^2 - 6x$ in completed square form.
(b) Write down the centre and radius of the circle $x^2 - 6x + y^2 = 7$.

*8 Find the centre and radius of these circles.
(a) $x^2 + y^2 - 20y = 21$
(b) $x^2 + 2x + y^2 - 4y = 4$

# 44 *Exactly so*

## Section A

1  The shapes below are drawn on a grid of centimetre squares.
   For each shape find, in terms of $\pi$,  (i) the perimeter  (ii) the area

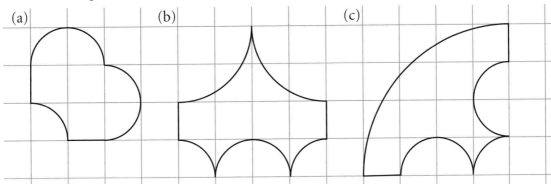

(a)    (b)    (c)

2  The diagram shows a running track.
   Find, in terms of $\pi$,

   (a)  the difference in length between the
        outer and inner edges of the track

   (b)  the area of the track (shaded)

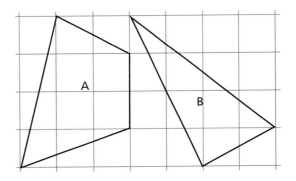

85 m

36 m          80 m

## Section B

1  These shapes are drawn on a grid of
   centimetre squares.

   (a)  Find, in surd form, the perimeter of
        quadrilateral A.

   (b)  Write the perimeter of triangle B in
        the form $a + b\sqrt{c}$, where $a$, $b$ and $c$
        are positive integers and $c$ is as small
        as possible.

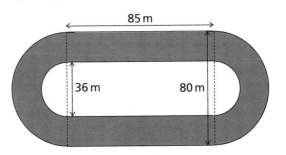

A

B

2  Find an exact expression for

   (a)  AC          (b)  AD

   (c)  the area of ABCD

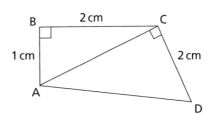

B    2 cm    C

1 cm          2 cm

A

D

## Section C

**1** A cylinder has radius 4 cm and height 5 cm.
Find, in terms of $\pi$,

    (a) the volume of the cylinder      (b) the total surface area of the cylinder

**2** A semicircle of radius 6 cm is made
(without overlapping) into the
curved surface of a cone.

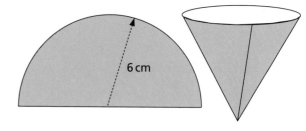

    (a) What is the radius of the 'base'
of the cone?

    (b) Find an expression for the
exact value of

        (i) the depth of the cone

        (ii) the volume of the cone

**\*3** Triangle ABC is an isosceles right-angled triangle.

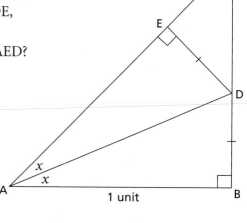

AD bisects the angle of 45° at A.
Because AD is the locus of points that are equidistant
from the lines AB and AC, it follows that DB = DE,
where DE is perpendicular to AC.

    (a) What can you say about triangles ABD and AED?

    (b) What is the length of AE?

    (c) Write the length AC in surd form.

    (d) Write the length EC in surd form.

    (e) Explain why EC = BD.

    (f) Use triangle ABD to find the value
of $\tan 22\frac{1}{2}°$ in surd form.

    (g) Use a calculator to find $\tan 22\frac{1}{2}°$ and
check the result agrees with (f).

**\*4** A rectangle of sides $a$ and $b$ is drawn inside a circle.
Semicircles are drawn on each of the four sides of
the rectangle, as shown here.

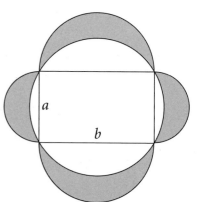

    (a) Explain why the area of the white circle is
$$\tfrac{1}{4}\pi(a^2 + b^2)$$

    (b) Show that the shaded area is equal to the area
of the rectangle.

# Mixed questions 11

1 Write these in order of size, smallest first.

$(\frac{4}{9})^0$ $\qquad$ $(\frac{4}{9})^{-1}$ $\qquad$ $(\frac{4}{9})^1$ $\qquad$ $(\frac{4}{9})^{\frac{1}{2}}$

2 In a survey of early morning traffic it was found that 55% of the vehicles on the road were commercial vehicles.
The ratio of male to female drivers of these commercial vehicles was 4 : 1.
For the non-commercial vehicles the ratio of male to female drivers was 4 : 5.

(a) For all the drivers involved in the survey, what was the ratio of males to females?

(b) If a commercial and a non-commercial driver were each chosen at random, what is the probability that they would be one male and one female?
Give your answer as a fraction in its simplest form.

3 A semicircle is removed from a quarter circle, as shown.
Prove that the shaded area remaining is
half the area of the original quarter circle.

4 The equation of a circle is $x^2 + y^2 = 13$.

(a) Write down the radius of the circle, in exact form.

(b) By solving a pair of simultaneous equations, find the coordinates of the points where the circle intersects the line $y = 2x - 1$.

5 In this diagram, AB is the diameter of the semicircle.

Find an expression for the exact value of

(a) the length AC

(b) the length BC

(c) the shaded area

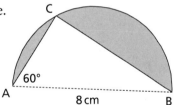

6 In the right-angled triangle PQR, PQ = 6.5 cm and QR = 4.6 cm.
Both measurements are correct to the nearest 0.1 cm.

Calculate upper and lower bounds for

(a) the length PR $\qquad$ (b) the area of PQR

(c) the tangent of angle QPR

7 Write down, as fractions, the reciprocals of $\qquad$ (a) $\frac{2}{3}$ $\qquad$ (b) 7 $\qquad$ (c) 0.3 $\qquad$ (d) 3.5

8 The diagram shows two right-angled triangles.

AD = 8 cm, sin $x$ = 0.7 and cos $y$ = 0.2.

Find BC.

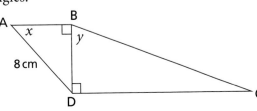

**9** The frequency polygon shows the times spent in a library by some visitors.

Calculate an estimate of the mean time these visitors spent in the library.

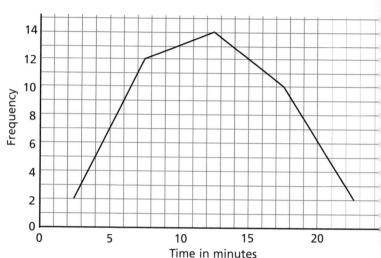

**10** Simplify these.

(a) $\dfrac{4a^2 - 12a}{a^2 - 9}$

(b) $\dfrac{4}{b - 2} - \dfrac{3}{b}$

(c) $\dfrac{5c^2}{3d} \div \dfrac{c^3}{9d^2}$

**11** The formula for the $n$th triangle number is $\frac{1}{2}n(n + 1)$.

(a) What is the sum of the 9th and 10th triangle numbers?

(b) Write down an expression for the $(n + 1)$th triangle number.

(c) Prove that adding two consecutive triangle numbers gives a square number.

**12** (a) Use congruent triangles to prove that opposite sides of a parallelogram are equal.

(b) PQRS is a parallelogram.
PX and RY are perpendicular to diagonal QS.
By using congruent triangles, prove that QX = SY.

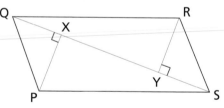

**13** The formula connecting $a$ and $c$ is given as $c = \dfrac{2a}{2 - ac}$.

(a) If $c = \frac{2}{5}$, find the value of $a$, giving your answer as a fraction in its simplest form.

(b) Make $a$ the subject of the formula.

**14** The sketch shows the position of three radio masts.

(a) Using a scale of 1 cm : 2 km draw the diagram accurately.

(b) Draw accurately the locus of all points equidistant from

(i) masts B and R (ii) masts E and R

(c) Mark with an X the position of the point that is equidistant from all three masts. Write down the distance from each of the masts to X.

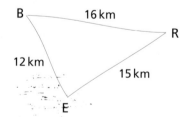

**15** Prove that the line $2x + y = 10$ does not intersect the circle $x^2 + y^2 = 15$.

**16** OACB is a parallelogram. $\overrightarrow{OA} = \mathbf{a}$ and $\overrightarrow{OB} = \mathbf{b}$.

X divides OC in the ratio $1:2$.

Y divides OC in the ratio $2:1$.

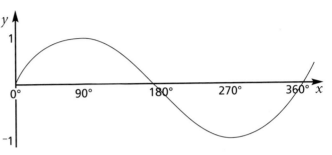

(a) Write expressions, in terms of **a** and **b**, for

(i) $\overrightarrow{OC}$  (ii) $\overrightarrow{OX}$  (iii) $\overrightarrow{OY}$

(iv) $\overrightarrow{BX}$  (v) $\overrightarrow{YA}$

(b) Prove that AXBY is a parallelogram.

**17** The graph is a sketch of $y = \sin x$ for $0° \le x \le 360°$.

(a) One solution to the equation $\sin x = {}^-0.3$ is $x = 197°$ to the nearest degree. Write down the other solution to the equation in the range $0° \le x \le 360°$.

(b) On separate diagrams sketch the graphs of

(i) $y = \sin x + 2$  (ii) $y = {}^-\sin x$  (iii) $y = 2\sin 2x$

**18** In the diagram AD is a tangent to the circle.

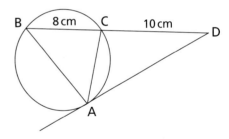

(a) Prove that triangles ABD and CAD are similar.

(b) Calculate the exact length of AD.

**19** (a) Expand and simplify $(x - 5)^2$.

(b) The expression $2x^2 - 20x + 53$ can be written in the form $2(x - a)^2 + b$. Find the values of $a$ and $b$.

(c) What is the minimum value of $2x^2 - 20x + 53$?

*20 The distance from the Earth to the Sun is $1.5 \times 10^8$ kilometres. Estimate the speed of the Earth, in both km/h and m/s, in its orbit round the Sun, stating clearly any assumptions that you have made.

*21 The diagram shows two concentric circles. The chord of the larger circle is a tangent to the smaller circle. The chord is 8 cm long. Find, in terms of $\pi$, the area of the shaded ring.

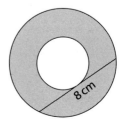

# 45 Rational and irrational numbers

## Sections A, B and C

1 Write these fractions as decimals.

(a) $\frac{12}{25}$  (b) $\frac{17}{20}$  (c) $\frac{7}{8}$  (d) $\frac{13}{40}$  (e) $\frac{9}{80}$

2 Which of these fractions are equivalent to terminating decimals?

$\frac{7}{30}$  $\frac{5}{32}$  $\frac{13}{90}$  $\frac{8}{27}$  $\frac{9}{40}$  $\frac{1}{45}$  $\frac{11}{75}$  $\frac{5}{7}$  $\frac{9}{80}$

3 Write these fractions as decimals.

(a) $\frac{2}{9}$  (b) $\frac{4}{11}$  (c) $\frac{3}{7}$  (d) $\frac{5}{13}$  (e) $\frac{7}{60}$

4 Write these decimals as fractions, in their simplest form.

(a) 0.45  (b) 0.135  (c) 0.45454545...  (d) $0.\dot{5}$  (e) $0.\dot{1}\dot{2}$

5 Write these decimals as fractions, in their simplest form.

(a) 0.3888888...  (b) $0.1\dot{5}$  (c) $0.05\dot{2}$  (d) $0.4\dot{5}4\dot{3}$

6 (a) Write $0.\dot{7}$ as a fraction.

(b) Write 0.2 as a fraction.

(c) Hence write $0.5\dot{7}$ as a fraction.

7 Which of these numbers are irrational?

$1.\dot{3}$   $\sqrt{10}$   $2\pi$   $\frac{22}{7}$   $\sqrt{49}$   $\sqrt[3]{27}$   4.93172   $\sqrt[3]{5}$   $\sqrt[3]{9}$

8 Simplify these.

(a) $\sqrt{3} + \sqrt{3}$  (b) $4(\sqrt{3} + 5)$  (c) $7\sqrt{5} - 3\sqrt{5}$
(d) $(\sqrt{6})^2$  (e) $(2\sqrt{5} + \sqrt{6}) + (3\sqrt{5} - 2\sqrt{6})$  (f) $(4\sqrt{3} + 5) - (\sqrt{3} - 4)$

9 Write down an irrational number between 6 and 7.

10 What is the exact length of side $x$ of this triangle?

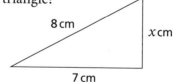

11 The sum of the reciprocals of two consecutive numbers is $0.1\dot{9}\dot{0}$.
Find the numbers.

## Sections D and E

1 Simplify these.

  (a) $\sqrt{5} \times \sqrt{7}$      (b) $2\sqrt{5} \times \sqrt{5}$      (c) $\sqrt{2} \times \sqrt{8}$      (d) $3\sqrt{5} \times 2\sqrt{6}$

Simplify each expression in questions 2 to 5, writing each one in the form $a\sqrt{b}$ where $a$ and $b$ are integers and $b$ is as small as possible.

2 (a) $\sqrt{20}$      (b) $\sqrt{75}$      (c) $\sqrt{90}$      (d) $\sqrt{54}$      (e) $\sqrt{250}$

  (f) $2\sqrt{24}$      (g) $5\sqrt{8}$      (h) $2\sqrt{40}$      (i) $5\sqrt{128}$      (j) $5\sqrt{700}$

3 (a) $\sqrt{3} \times \sqrt{6}$      (b) $\sqrt{5} \times \sqrt{35}$      (c) $\sqrt{20} \times \sqrt{10}$      (d) $\sqrt{21} \times \sqrt{7}$

4 (a) $\sqrt{3} + \sqrt{12}$      (b) $\sqrt{125} - 2\sqrt{5}$      (c) $\sqrt{60} - \sqrt{15}$      (d) $2\sqrt{80} - \sqrt{45}$

5 (a) $\frac{\sqrt{40}}{2}$      (b) $\frac{\sqrt{50}}{\sqrt{2}}$      (c) $\frac{6}{\sqrt{6}}$      (d) $\frac{\sqrt{150}}{5}$      (e) $\frac{\sqrt{48}}{2}$

6 Multiply out the brackets and simplify these.

  (a) $(2 + \sqrt{5})(2 + \sqrt{5})$      (b) $(6 - \sqrt{2})(1 + \sqrt{2})$      (c) $(5 + \sqrt{3})^2$

7 What is the area of a square of side $(2 + \sqrt{3})$?

  Give your answer in the form $a + b\sqrt{3}$.

8 (a) Simplify these.

    (i) $(\sqrt{7} + \sqrt{2})(\sqrt{7} - \sqrt{2})$      (ii) $(\sqrt{5} + \sqrt{20})^2$      (iii) $(\sqrt{8} - \sqrt{2})(\sqrt{12} + \sqrt{2})$

  (b) Which of your answers to (a) are irrational?

9 Write $(\sqrt{10} + \sqrt{2})^2$ in the form $a + b\sqrt{c}$ where $c$ is as small as possible.

10 (a) If $x = \sqrt{10} - 2$ find the value of $x^2$ in the form $a + b\sqrt{c}$.

  (b) Hence, or otherwise, show that $\sqrt{10} - 2$ is a solution to the equation

     $x^2 + 4x - 6 = 0$

11 A large square encloses two smaller squares as shown. The smaller squares have areas $3\,\text{cm}^2$ and $5\,\text{cm}^2$.

  (a) Write down the exact length of a side of the largest square.

  (b) Work out the area of the largest square, writing your answer in the form $a + b\sqrt{c}$.

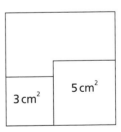

12 (a) Find, in surd form, the length labelled $a$.

  (b) Do the same for $b$ and explain why $b = 2a$.

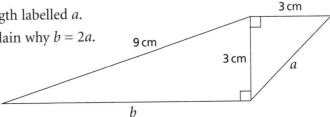

## Sections F and G

1 Simplify these.

(a) $\dfrac{\sqrt{20}}{\sqrt{5}}$    (b) $\dfrac{\sqrt{32}}{\sqrt{2}}$    (c) $\dfrac{\sqrt{21}}{\sqrt{3}}$

2 Evaluate these.

(a) $\sqrt{\dfrac{16}{49}}$    (b) $\sqrt{\dfrac{1}{25}}$    (c) $\sqrt{\dfrac{4}{81}}$    (d) $\sqrt{\dfrac{64}{9}}$

3 Write $\sqrt{\dfrac{7}{25}}$ in the form $\dfrac{\sqrt{a}}{b}$ where $a$ and $b$ are integers.

4 Write each expression with an integer denominator and in its simplest form.

(a) $\dfrac{2}{\sqrt{3}}$    (b) $\dfrac{1}{\sqrt{5}}$    (c) $\dfrac{11}{\sqrt{11}}$    (d) $\dfrac{\sqrt{7}}{\sqrt{2}}$    (e) $\dfrac{\sqrt{6}}{\sqrt{5}}$

5 Show that $\dfrac{\sqrt{3}}{5} + \dfrac{1}{\sqrt{3}}$ is equal to $\dfrac{8\sqrt{3}}{15}$.

6 (a) Find the exact value of the diameter of this circle.

(b) Write down the radius of the circle.

(c) Find the exact value of the area of the circle.

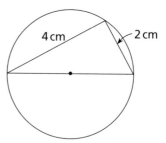

7 Rita thinks that if two irrational numbers are added the answer will always be irrational. Give an example to show when this is not true.

8 Write $0.01\dot{2}$ as a fraction in its simplest form.

9 Which of the following are irrational?

$(\sqrt{7})^2$    $\sqrt{5} - 2$    $\sqrt{28} \times \sqrt{14}$    $(\sqrt{5} - 2)(\sqrt{5} + 2)$    $\dfrac{\sqrt{12}}{\sqrt{3}}$    $\sqrt{24} - \sqrt{6}$

10 (a) Evaluate  (i) $\sqrt{6\frac{1}{4}}$    (ii) $\sqrt{0.01}$

(b) Write $\sqrt{2\frac{2}{9}}$ in the form $\dfrac{a\sqrt{b}}{c}$ where $a$, $b$ and $c$ are integers.

11 The diagram shows a square with the quadrant of a circle shaded. The area of the square is $6\,\text{cm}^2$.

What is the exact value of the shaded area?

12 Solve the equation $x^2 - 6x + 1 = 0$ giving your solutions in the form $a \pm b\sqrt{c}$.

# 46 *Further trigonometry*

## Sections B and C

**1** Find each missing length to 1 d.p.

(a)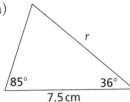

(b)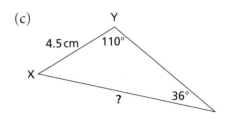

(c)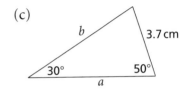

**2** Find the lengths marked with letters.

(a)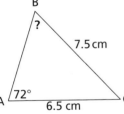

(b)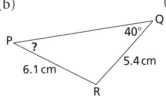

(c)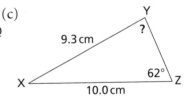

**3** Find the missing angle in each triangle, to the nearest degree.
Make sure that the angle you give is possible for that triangle.
If there are two possible angles, give them both.

(a)

(b)

(c)

**4** The diagram shows a metal framework.

(a) Find length AC.

(b) Angle ADC is obtuse.
Find the size of angle ADC.

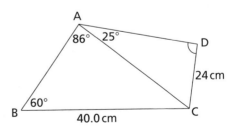

## Section D

**1** Find each missing length to 1 d.p.

(a)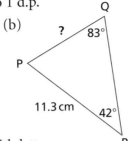

(b)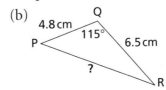

(c)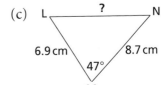

**2** Use the cosine rule to find the missing angles, to the nearest degree.

(a)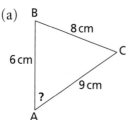

(b)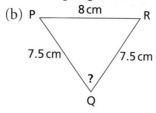

(c)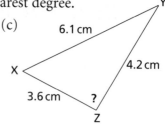

**3** Five small planes are flying in V formation.
The distance from the pilot of the leading plane to each of the pilots of the planes at the back is 250 m.
The angle between the two 'arms' of the V is 75°.

How far apart are the two back pilots?

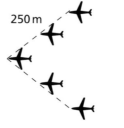

## Sections E and F

**1** Find the area of each of these shapes.

(a)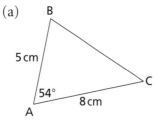

(b)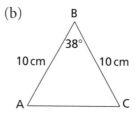

(c)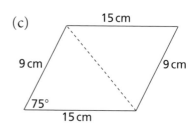

**2** The area of this rhombus is 120 cm².

(a) Find the acute angle marked x.

(b) Find the length of the shorter diagonal of the rhombus.

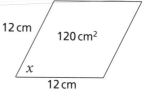

**3** Two surveyors stand at points A and B, 45 m apart on a straight road.
They each record the angle between the road and their line of sight to a tree, as shown in the diagram.

(a) Calculate the distance between surveyor A and the tree.

(b) Calculate the shortest distance from the road to the tree.

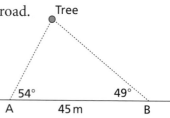

**4** Town B is 10 km due north of town A.
Town C is 12 km from A and has bearing 068° from A.
Find the distance and bearing of town C from town B.

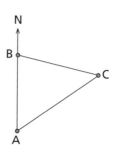

# 47 Three dimensions

## Sections A, B and C

1 Each grid here is a grid of unit squares.
Calculate the following, giving your answers
correct to two decimal places.

  (a) AB         (b) AC

  (c) The angle between line AB and line AC

  (d) The angle between line AC and plane OBCE

  (e) AD       (f) DC      (g) angle CAD

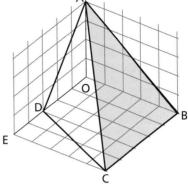

2 A pole of height 5.2 m is kept vertical by three 'guy ropes'.
Each guy rope is fixed to the top of the pole and to a point
on level ground 2.4 m from the base of the pole.
The three points where the ropes are fixed to the ground
form an equilateral triangle.

Calculate these, correct to 1 d.p.

  (a) The length of each rope

  (b) The angle each rope makes with the ground

  (c) The length of each side of the equilateral triangle

  (d) The angle between any pair of ropes

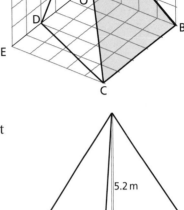

3 Square ABCD, of side 10 cm, is inclined
at an angle of 22° to the horizontal.
Point E on AB is 4 cm from A and 6 cm from B.

Calculate these, correct to the nearest 0.1°.

  (a) The angle between EC and the horizontal

  (b) The angle between ED and the horizontal

  (c) The angle between EC and ED

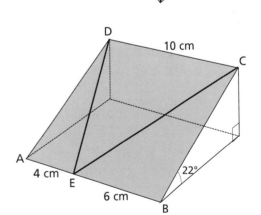

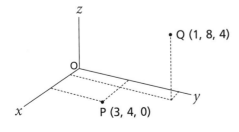

4 Calculate the following.

  (a) The distance PQ

  (b) The angle between PQ and the
$xy$ plane, to the nearest 0.1°

# Mixed questions 12

1 Write each of these as a fraction in its simplest form.

(a) $0.5\dot{4}$          (b) $0.\dot{3}2\dot{1}$          (c) $0.4\dot{8}$

2 Two representatives are to be chosen from a group of four girls and four boys.
The eight names are put into a box and two are drawn at random.
Calculate the probability that a boy and a girl will be chosen.

3 Solve these equations.

(a) $\dfrac{x}{2} - \dfrac{x-1}{3} = 4$          (b) $\dfrac{2}{x} - \dfrac{1}{x-1} = 6$

4 Find the lowest integer value of $n$ for which $1 - 5n < 12 - 2n$.

5 Write $(3 + \sqrt{5})(2 + \sqrt{20})$ in the form $p + q\sqrt{r}$, where $p$, $q$ and $r$ are positive integers and $r$ is as small as possible.

6 This cone has base radius 12 cm and
curved surface area $156\pi$ cm$^2$.
Find, in terms of $\pi$, the volume of the cone.

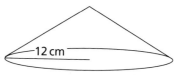

7 A, B and C are three points on level ground.
B is 325 m due north of A.
C is 570 m from A on a bearing of 108° from A.

Calculate these.

(a) Area ABC, to the nearest 10 m$^2$

(b) Distance BC, to the nearest metre

(c) The bearing of C from B, to the nearest 0.1°

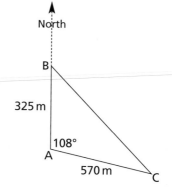

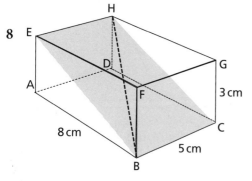

8 The diagram shows a cuboid ABCDEFGH whose
edges are of length 8 cm, 5 cm and 3 cm.

Calculate the following.

(a) The angle between the plane BCHE and the
base ABCD

(b) The length of the diagonal BH

(c) The angle between BH and the plane CDHG

9 The sides of a triangle are of length 8 cm, 7 cm and 5 cm.
Calculate the size of the largest angle of the triangle.

10 Quantities $X$ and $Y$ are known to be connected by an equation of the form $Y = aX^2 + b$.

| $X$ | 0.8 | 1.0 | 1.3 | ... |
|---|---|---|---|---|
| $Y$ | 4.9 | ... | 15.4 | 30.9 |

Calculate

(a) the values of $a$ and $b$    (b) the missing values in the table

11 (a) The expression $x^2 - 14x + a$ can be written in the form $(x - b)^2$. Find the values of $a$ and $b$.

(b) Solve the equation $x^2 - 14x + 15 = 0$, giving your answer in the form $c \pm \sqrt{d}$.

(c) State the minimum value of $x^2 - 14x + 15$.

12 Triangle PQR is right-angled at Q. QS is perpendicular to PR.

(a) Explain why triangles PQR, QSR and PSQ are similar.

(b) Calculate the length of PS.

(c) Find in the form $a : b : c$, where $a$, $b$ and $c$ are integers and are as small as possible, the ratio area triangle QSR : area triangle PSQ : area triangle PQR.

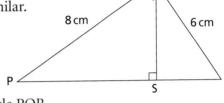

13 The diagram shows a solid consisting of a cylinder and a hemisphere. The cylinder and hemisphere have radius 9 cm.

The volume of the solid is 13 850 cm³.

Find the total height of the solid.

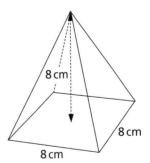

14 The weight of a disc cut from a metal sheet is proportional to the square of the diameter. A disc of diameter 5.8 cm weighs 268 g.

Calculate, to a reasonable degree of accuracy,

(a) the weight of a disc of diameter 7.4 cm

(b) the diameter of a disc that weighs 164 g

15 A square-based pyramid has a base 8 cm square and a height of 8 cm.

Calculate, to two significant figures,

(a) the length of each sloping edge

(b) the area of each sloping face

(c) the angle between each sloping face and the base

(d) the angle between each sloping edge and the base

16 (a) Find the coordinates of the points of intersection of the line $y + 2x = 5$ and the circle $x^2 + y^2 = 50$.

(b) Find the length of the chord joining these two points of intersection, giving your answer in the form $a\sqrt{b}$, where $a$ and $b$ are integers with $b$ as small as possible.

**17** The diagram shows a sector of a circle of radius 12 mm. The angle of the sector is 40°.

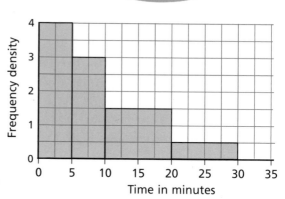

(a) Calculate the perimeter of the sector.

(b) Calculate the area of the shaded segment.

**18** This histogram shows the distribution of consultation times in a medical practice one day.

(a) How many consultations lasted no more than 5 minutes?

(b) What percentage of consultations lasted 10 minutes or more?

(c) Estimate the mean length of a consultation, showing your working.

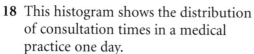

**19** A rectangular garden 10 m by 8 m has a path of width $x$ m round the inside edge. Inside the path is a flower bed (shaded).

(a) Find an expression in terms of $x$ for the area of the flower bed.

(b) Find, to 2 d.p., the value of $x$ for which the area of the flower bed is half of the area of the garden.

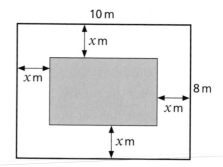

**✗*20** (a) Find the area of the shaded square.

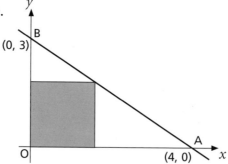

(b) AB touches the circle at T.
OT is a diameter of the circle.
Find, in terms of $\pi$, the area of the circle.

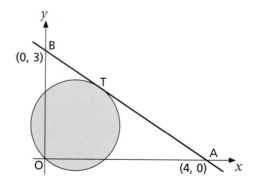